STEPHEN McGINTY

CHURCHILL'S CIGAR

PAN BOOKS

First published 2007 by Macmillan

First published in paperback 2008 by Pan Books
an imprint of Pan Macmillan Ltd
Pan Macmillan, 20 New Wharf Road, London N1 9RR
Basingstoke and Oxford
Associated companies throughout the world
www.panmacmillan.com

ISBN 978-0-330-46121-4

A CIP catalogue record for this book is available from
the British Library.

Typeset by Intype Libra Ltd
Printed and bound in the UK by
CPI Mackays, Chatham ME5 8TD

FOR MY L. A. WOMAN

ACKNOWLEDGEMENTS

The idea for *Churchill's Cigar* was sparked while reading Piers Brendon's excellent introduction to our greatest Prime Minister *Churchill: A Brief Life* in which he wrote of the vastness of the Churchill archives and commented on the number of files on his cigars alone. I have had the opportunity to thank him in person and now shall do so in print.

My own path through the labyrinth of the archives at Churchill College, Cambridge University, was smoothed by the facility's dedicated staff, in particular I would like to thank Andrew Riley and Caroline Herbert for assistance in securing photographs and, in particular, the centre's director, Allen Packwood, whose article, 'Protecting the Premier', in his Finest Hour, first pointed me in the direction of the team assembled to defend Churchill from any rogue cigars.

A figure of crucial assistance in writing this book was Phil Reed, director of the Churchill Museum and Cabinet War Rooms, who not only introduced me to the Prime Minister's former staff but generously agreed to read the manuscript prior to publication. I might add that any errors that slipped past are entirely my responsibility. I would also like to thank his colleague, Sarah Clarke, for assistance in choosing photographs. It was at the launch of the museum that I was first introduced to Churchill's former staff including Patrick Kinna, Lady Williams, Doreen Pugh and Elizabeth Nel and his grandson, Winston S. Churchill, who all gave freely of their time to assist me in this project, while at a later function I met and spoke with Lady Soames, his daughter. A special mention must go to Sir Anthony Montague Browne, Churchill's last private secretary, and his charming wife, Shelagh, for an excellent interview and tasty shepherd's pie.

Anyone who writes about Winston Churchill is indebted to the Herculean labours of Sir Martin Gilbert, his official historian, who I thank for his interview and choice anecdote. I would also like to thank Andrew

Roberts, John Keegan, David Reynolds and John Ramsden for their own inspiring works.

Robert Emery, director of James J. Fox & Robert Lewis, allowed me access to the shop's ledgers and Churchill memorabilia, while Peter Tiley, director of the Dunhill Museum and Archive, was also generous with his time and materials. Thanks also go to Judith Seaward, who escorted me round Chartwell.

In America, I would like to thank Marvin R. Shanken and Gordon Mott of *Cigar Aficionado*, organizers of the Las Vegas Big Smoke, and Brian Dempsey, for friendship and providing accommodation and a space to write in Santa Monica.

In Cuba I was assisted by Steve Gibbs of the BBC, Jorge Jorge, Jorge J. Fernandez, my indomitable fixer William Rakip, Adriano Martinez Rius, author of *Habano the King* and *The Great Habano Factories*, Jose Antonio Candia and Lic. Manuel Garcia at Habanos S.A. and Michael E. Parmly, chief of mission, who was generous enough to give me a guided tour of the American ambassador's residence in Havana where Churchill once dined.

Perhaps the biggest single champion of this book was Simon Chase, marketing director of Hunters & Frankau, who, along with his colleagues David Lewis, Jemma

Freeman, Philip Hambidge and Anna Lopez gave generously of their time and wide knowledge of the cigar trade. I'm deeply grateful.

The last few years would have been more difficult without the support of the staff of the *Scotsman* newspaper, including the editor, Mike Gilson, the cigar-puffing deputy editor, Ian Stewart, and Paul Riddell. I would also like to add my appreciation of Frank O'Donnell and James Hall on the news desk, all the library staff and my fellow toilers in the Glasgow office, Craig Brown, Alastair Dalton, Emma Cowing, Andrew Eaton and Sandra Quinn.

For general enthusiasm and encouragement I would like to thank David Wylie, Frank Deasy and Thomas Quinn. At Macmillan I thank my editors, Richard Milner, Georgina Difford and Jean Maund. Special thanks must go to my agent, Eddie Bell, who never lost faith in this project.

I would like to thank my brother, Paul, sisters, Claire and Alison, nephew, Charlie, and my parents, Margaret and Frank, and my mother-in-law, Sarah Anderson, who served the war effort by building engines at the Rolls Royce factory in Glasgow.

Last in the acknowledgements but, of course, first in my life I would like to thank my wife, Lori, for putting up with me as I toiled in my shed.

CONTENTS

PREFACE

'There is no question of Winston Churchill's
place in the cigar smoker's pantheon . . .'

Gordon Mott,
executive editor of *Cigar Aficionado*.

THE SCENT OF cigar smoke has the ability to perfume the air at a remarkable distance from where the lit end softly glows. Multiply a solitary smoker by 4,000 and it is no wonder that guests at 'The Big Smoke', held in the Mandalay Bay casino and convention centre in Las Vegas, have little need for the brightly decorated signs that offer directions towards the evening's entertainment. They just follow their noses.

For an hour, men in brush-cut hairstyles, complemented by thick moustaches and clothed in the executive wardrobe of play – white sneakers, chino-style shorts and button-down shirts – have marched along the corridors of this vast metropolis. They have skirted round the vegetation that resembles a caged rain-forest, passed the shark reef with its crowd-pulling tiger sharks and listened to the soulless trill of the one-arm bandits, designed of course to rob with the skill of two. A few are accompanied by women: blondes in their forties, brunettes in their thirties, and even the occasional young girl for whom lighting up would, judging by appearance, seem an illegal act. Many are smoking. The women puff on short robustos, the men favouring cigars that more closely resemble a cedar log. It is an act, in a public building, which in any other city would be grounds for arrest or fine, but in Las Vegas – where you can lose your house on red before comforting yourself in the capacious chest of a lap dancer – smoking, particularly ostentatious cigars, is positively encouraged. Caesar's Palace even has an advert that spoofs the anti-smoking lobby. A beautiful, dark-eyed temptress reclines in a leather armchair and pushes a thick cigar between her ruby lips. The caption reads: 'smoking Permitted'.

The corridors of the hotel's convention centre are so vast that a guest would benefit from a golf cart to traverse them. And yet by 6.25 p.m., on a Friday evening in November 2004, one long corridor was packed with 4,000 cigar lovers, many puffing out little clouds of blue-tinged smoke as they waited patiently for entry to the first of the weekend's 'Big Smoke' events. Inside the main conference centre, a huge room the size of a foot-ball field, there was a bustle of last-minute activity. Each of the twenty-one cigar manufacturers had their stalls decorated, their free samples to hand and their eye-candy: young ladies with brilliant white teeth, long slender legs, and ample cleavage squeezed into the tightest of tops. Organized by the magazine *Cigar Aficionado*, as a means of both celebrating the cigar and introducing new brands to the consumer, 'The Big Smoke' is really an opportunity for like-minded obses-sives to toast (or perhaps roast) their pastime.

Upon entry each guest receives a canvas shopping bag printed with the *Cigar Aficionado* logo, and a book of numbered tickets. Each number corresponds to a cigar stall where it can be exchanged for a free sample. While the stalls remain at the heart of the vast room, the essential accoutrements that constitute 'the good life' float before your eyes, like smoke itself. Jaguar, Mercedes and the mammoth military-style Hummer cars are on display. In one booth, surrounded by white netting, a golf pro coaches the perfect swing. At another, a long line of largely overweight men with an abundant variety of facial hair queue up to stand against a blue screen and have their protruding cigar lit by the Monte-cristo Platinum Girl. She is a beautiful nude model, encased in silver body paint, who appears in a series of popular adverts for Montecristo Platinum cigars, a quality brand produced by Altadis USA Cigars, the largest manufacturer in the United States. She's also a collection of pixels, for the men are photographed on their own and the 'girl' added afterwards by computer. The only stall with a longer queue is the one where enthusiasts receive a photo and an iron-clad handshake from a physically present legend of American football.

It is curious to think what Winston Churchill, the secular saint of the cigar smoker, would make of this jamboree. After all, he is the man who embodied the trinity of values, strength, power and wealth, or in his case the illusion of wealth, which are today most associated with this rolled collection of tobacco leaves. Would he wrinkle his nose at so many fit young men at leisure at a time of 'war'? Perhaps, but then again, perhaps not. After all, the 'war on terror' is as nothing to the total war through which the British Prime Minister led his country in 1940–1945. He might have liked the scene. Churchill, remember, loved Americans in all their manners. The son of an American mother whom he adored (though she made little time for him), he made frequent tours of the country before and after the war. During the conflict he requested that America 'give us the tools and we will finish the job'. No one was more relieved, however, when after Pearl Harbor, America rolled up its sleeves and joined in.

In fact, there is evidence to suggest that Winston would have been tickled pink to spend a few hours in such a place. Certainly he may in fact have favoured Pol Roger champagne, but there were the finest Californian wines, red and white, and brandy by the goblet. For a man with a hearty appetite, the plates of rare roast beef, seared lobster and fresh pasta on offer would have been too small, though that problem could be solved by stacking them together. As a politician he had always taken a childish delight in the latest inventions, which in the early decades of the twentieth century included planes and helicopters. So the display of the Hummer, designed for use in the deserts such as in Iraq (a country Churchill himself had a hand in creating), now kitted out with leather interiors and in-built DVD players for soccer moms and wannabe 'bad' dads, would have had him climbing aboard for a swift spin.

There were also scenes which would not have met with his approval. A devoted family man with little interest in, or regard for, the fairer sex beyond his beloved wife Clementine and his daughters, the presence of dancers – tame by Las Vegas standards but dressed in fishnet tights, black boots and black bras – would have had him spluttering his disapproval. Yet as a man who adored the casinos of Monte Carlo (on one occasion he lost a considerable sum, much to the chagrin of his wife), the lure of the crap tables, roulette and the soft green baize two floors below might have been enough for him to extend his personal benediction on the event. This is only what we can imagine. What is for certain is the regard in which cigar smokers of the world continue to hold Winston Churchill.

'Winston Churchill – now there was a man who loved his cigars,' said Ron, a tall, angular man with a thick head of salt-and-pepper hair and a fondness for Cao cigars. A regular attender at 'Big Smoke' events, he continued: 'I think he's the perfect ambassador for the cigar smoker. He represents the best of what we want to be. He was a man of taste, and talent, but whose greatest achievement was his tenacity. He never gave in. That's what we need, tenacity, against these bastards who want to stub out our passion.'

Gordon Mott is the executive editor of *Cigar Aficionado* and host of the weekend's event. In a quiet corner of an outside corridor, he sits in an overstuffed armchair, puffs on a cigar and ruminates on Churchill. 'There is no question of Winston Churchill's place in the cigar-smoker's pantheon. He's one of the only men to grace the cover of the magazine twice and he was voted our man of the century.' The editorial for that issue asked, 'Has anyone ever embodied the pleasures of cigar smoking more than he did? Has anyone ever seen a photograph of Churchill without his constant companion?'

The cigar business in America has gone through a revolution in the past fifteen years. When Winston Churchill died in 1965 sales of cigars in America were at an all time high of nine billion, the vast majority of which were poor quality and machine rolled. Sales of quality, hand-rolled cigars accounted for just 5 per cent of the market (450 million). By the 1980s the number of imported cigars was virtually flat at 100 million, and retailers were grateful if their sales dropped by only two or three per cent annually. The sum spent on advertising quality cigars was indicative of the market's stagnation: just $1 million per year.

The launch of *Cigar Aficionado* in September 1992 corresponded to or, according to its publisher, Marvin Shanken, triggered the first rise in the market for decades. In 1993 premium cigar imports to the USA rose by 10 per cent. In 1994 the figure was 12.4 per cent. Then, like a fat cigar on a steep incline, the market growth picked up speed. In 1995 imports rose by 33.1 per cent; in 1996 by 66.6 per cent and, finally, in 1997 by 76.8 per cent, which represented a total of 520 million cigars. Of course, a rise is often succeeded by a fall, and so it was in the cigar business. The boom, while not quite going bust, certainly leaked a lot of air. In a bid to meet escalating orders, cigar manufacturers used lower-grade tobacco which resulted in inconsistent smokes. Over the next five years sales dropped to around 253.3 million in 2002, a disappointing figure compared with 1997 but still an increase of 250 per cent in a decade.

Yet a curious mood has emerged. A new frisson of resistance has rippled across the country. The health battle against smokers was handed an extra weapon in its armoury in January 1993 when the Environmental Protection Agency reported that 'second-hand smoke' killed 3,000 non-smokers each year.* From this report flowed a tide of anti-smoking legislation. Five years later California became the first state to ban smoking in public places. Other states which followed included

*A federal judge would later repudiate the EPA's report, suggesting that the Agency had manipulated, misrepresented and exaggerated the data.

Florida and New York. In Europe countries such as Ireland and Italy followed suit, with Scotland becoming smoke-free in 2006 and with England and Wales stubbing out in the summer of 2007. Yet still the cigar burns on.

The cigar was integral to the character of Winston Churchill. In November 2005, the publishers Hutchinson issued a short book about Isambard Kingdom Brunel, the Victorian engineer, who was also an inveterate cigar smoker. They erased the cigar from a classic portrait of him, and insisted it was not a major part of his character – unlike, they explained, the character of Winston Churchill.

The aim of this short book is simple. To trace the smoke signals from the first contented puff by the Greatest Briton (as voted by viewers of the BBC) on the recreation that would define, if glimpsed in silhouette, his character. To ask what cigars meant to him, what risks he would undertake to smoke them, and what was it about burning tobacco that brought ease and balance to a mind and body forced – through Nazi aggression and American reticence – to carry the last hope of a democratic Europe.

Since taking his first puffs as a schoolboy and experiencing Cuban cigars in Havana as a young war correspondent amid the battles of the Spanish-Cuban war in 1895, until his death seventy years later, Winston Churchill was rarely without a cigar clamped between his jaws. His cigar became a potent political prop, a handy pointer and steady source of solace when the 'Black Dog' of depression snapped at his heels. Whether he smoked seven each day, beginning at breakfast, 200,000 during his lifetime, or as his daughter Mary Soames suggested: 'not as many as people thought', the Prime Minister was defined by his private passion, inspired two generations of cigar smokers and bequeathed the world the Churchill, one of the largest and most impressive cigars.

Churchill's Cigar charts the politician's relationship with his cigar and the men such as Samuel Kaplan, a New York well-wisher who kept him in supplies during the Second World War and created the first 'Churchill' cigar. Or Antonio Giraudier, a Cuban millionaire who for almost twenty years took on the role of filling Churchill's humidor, even after he was forced to flee his native land following Castro's revolution.

The book examines the extraordinary lengths, supervised by Lord Rothschild, that were taken during the war to ensure the Prime Minister was not poisoned by a rogue cigar. It also traces his passion through his various flirtations with different brands, styles and sizes with which he regularly experimented, and examine the clandestine system that left suppliers unaware of each other. It also explores how the constant infusions of nicotine affected the balance of his mind. We meet artists such as the photographer Yousuf Karsh, who achieved his classic photograph of a scowling Churchill by snatching the cigar from his mouth, and Clare Sheridan, the sculptor who threatened to commit suicide on the steps of No. 10 Downing Street unless the Prime Minister gave her a ten-minute sitting without the cigar.

Following his death in 1965 Churchill's relationship with cigars continued with the creation of the eponymous cigar and the erection, in the new Australian town of Churchill, of a 101-foot bronze 'cigar' (see Chapter 6). Even today, forty years after his death, the trade in his cigar accoutrements remains increasingly fierce. Who, for instance, would spend £43,000 for his gold cigar case or £2,270 for his cigar stub? Even fellow cigar lovers, such as Groucho Marx, were intrigued by his passion:

One night at the embassy Winston Churchill's daughter Mary was my dinner partner. When the butler passed round the cigars, she said, 'Take one for me.' I said, 'What? What do you want a cigar for? You don't smoke cigars, do you?' She said, 'No, but my father does, Winston, and we play a little game.' I said, 'What kind of a game?' 'I take a cigar, and he takes a cigar, and then he bets me a pound' – I think it was around two and a half dollars – 'and we bet who can hold the ash on the cigar the longest.' At this time he was running the British Government. Now, you never think of a man like that trying to win two bucks from his daughter.

So come, let us follow the smoke.

ONE

CIGARS, YOUNG WINSTON AND ROBERT LEWIS

'You do not like my smoking cigars.
I will not do so anymore, I am not fond enough
of them in having any difficulty in leaving them off.'

Winston Churchill, in a letter to his father,
27 October 1893.

A T THE BIRTH of the twentieth century, Hansom cab drivers in London would receive a pouch full of shag for every customer safely delivered to Robert Lewis, the tobacconist at 81 St James's Street. A small barrel of loose tobacco was placed just inside the front entrance, so that cabbies could escort their charges inside, scoop up their sweet-scented bonus and return swiftly to the reins. However, Winston Churchill did not require a Victorian cabbie to introduce him to the wood-panelled interior of the capital's premier tobacconist. Robert Lewis was located on St James's Street, a boulevard dedicated to gentlemen's clubs and shops that catered to the requirements of their clientele, such as saddlers, gunmakers, and coffee houses where the political gossip was as scalding as the beverage being served. It could be assumed that Winston's father, Lord Randolph Churchill (a frequenter of the capital's clubs) had informed his son of Robert Lewis's location prior to his death from syphilis in 1895. Yet in fact it was his mother, Lady Churchill (formerly Jennie Jerome), a great American beauty who had carried her country's confidence to her new home. English ladies of the day would not have entered the shop, but Lady Churchill was a fan of the firm's gold-tipped Alexandra Balkan cigarettes, which she smoked using a small amber tube which cost one guinea.

On 9 August 1900, a hot and muggy summer's day, Winston Churchill, then twenty-five years old, first stepped into Robert Lewis and began a relationship that lasted sixty-five years and ended only with his death in 1965. In later life, as we shall see, Churchill was promiscuous with cigar retailers, secretly enjoying supplies from any number while leaving each with the perception that they were the chosen one. Robert Lewis, however, deserves the description as his most favoured establishment and has the heavy leather-bound order books as testament. On that first day young Winston purchased 50 Bock Giraldas, a small Havana cigar, for £4, and a box of 100 large Balkan cigarettes at a further cost of 11 shillings. It was an order he would repeat every couple of weeks for many years.

The interior of Robert Lewis was panelled with dark wood. The walls had floor-to-ceiling shelves on which sat neatly stacked boxes of cigarettes and cigars. Illumination was provided by parallel rows of floral-shaped lamps. To the right, as customers stepped through the door, was a long wooden counter on which pipe racks were displayed and where a solitary ashtray – regularly emptied – was placed. Behind the counter stood a wooden writing scribe with silver inkwell on which the ledger was regularly updated by Charles Craven, the store manager, a clean-shaven and carefully dressed man who possessed an air of aristocratic decorum. Like many stores of the time, Robert Lewis had its own commissionaire. Sergeant Major Rose was a tall, thin man with a carefully waxed moustache whose dark green uniform bore the medals he had earned as a veteran of the Rifle Brigade, which had participated in the 324-mile march from Kabul to Kandahar in August 1880 during the Second Anglo-Afghan War. Rose, who also acted as caretaker, lived in a small flat above the shop with his wife and three children. In 1900, a sixteen-year-old boy named Fred Croley joined the staff. A tall, quiet, thrifty character, he would become the right-hand man and future partner to the store's owner and guiding spirit, José de Solo Pinto.

On that Thursday in August 1900 when Winston Churchill arrived at the shop, Mr de Solo Pinto was absent. His beloved Scottish wife, Hannah Lawrence, was dying in the upstairs bedroom of the family's detached house in Hampstead and José, an emotional, charismatic Jew, was distraught. Not only was Hannah his life, and the mother of his two small children – May Abigail, seven, and Vivian, a boy of five – but she had helped to build his new livelihood. It was her employer, an affluent, strong-willed and intellectual Victorian spinster called Miss Semuda, who had lent José the necessary funds to purchase Robert Lewis Tobacconist in December 1898. Born in 1810, Miss Semuda had been a friend of Count D'Orsay and Alfred Guillaume Gabriel, the amateur artist and professional dandy, while her brother was a distinguished naval engineer and Liberal MP. Six years earlier, in 1892, she had agreed to José's request to marry Hannah, who worked as her paid companion, whereupon she in turn literally became a member of the new family. The large house in Greencroft Gardens was bought for the ample space that allowed Miss Semuda and her sister to move in, and at the age of ninety she was as distressed as José over

Hannah's deteriorating health. Hannah would succumb to cancer that August.

Before grief descended on his broad shoulders, José de Solo Pinto had the brash manner of a poor boy made good. Born among the Jewish community of the city's East End, he was tied to his race but not its faith. Although he would boast that the family name could be traced back to their eviction from Spain in the fifteenth century by King Ferdinand and Queen Isabella, he raised his son and daughter as Protestants rather than tolerate any interference by his family in their upbringing after their own mother's death. The success of Desola, his wholesale company, was largely in spite of rather than due to his management. He had a head for business that was buried in the sand and staff frequently referred to him as 'The Ostrich', a moniker of which he grew so fond that he frequently used it in correspondence.

José enjoyed the good life to a degree which would make his most famous customer doff his top hat in admiration – throwing expensive parties, dispensing lavish gifts and matching Winston Churchill glass for brimming glass. At breakfast he would consume a tumbler of sherry, lunch was accompanied by two bottles of wine and another two were downed at dinner, while copious glasses of port helped send him to sleep. When he discovered he had diabetes, then a common killer, he took out a life insurance policy worth £1 million which he paid for with a single large premium. When insulin was later developed and his life was no longer in the balance, he resented the cost of his policy until the day he died. Yet instead of modifying his diet to suit his disease, he examined the day's menu and, assisted by his barber-surgeon, who arrived at the family home each morning to shave him, the pair worked out what insulin was required to keep him out of a diabetic coma while he consumed meals with gusto.

Robert Lewis the store had been purchased by Pinto in 1898 following the retirement of Charles Edward Baxter and the death of William Hanson Dodswell, its previous proprietors, who had helped to assure the shop's success by signing a lucrative deal with the founder of the game of lawn tennis. Major Walter Clopton Wingfield, who wrote his guide to the game in 1874, was an inveterate inventor who pioneered the less successful sport of bicycle gymkhana (formation cycling to classical music) as well as a popular pipe mixture. The major sold the secret recipe and licence to Robert Lewis in 1886 – demanding and receiving not just a handsome sum but a copy of the tobacco tin made from silver 'of about the thickness of a shilling' plus a lifetime's supply of his eponymous pipe weed to be delivered to his door each week.

The store can be traced back through multiple hands and round a variety of addresses to a small site at 14 Long Acre in Covent Garden, opened in 1787 by a young Welshman by the name of Christopher Lewis. He had arrived in the capital a few years earlier and experimented with various trades before settling on being sa tobacconist. The area provided local shops for the inhabitants of the stone mansions of the Strand, yet despite being in a potentially profitable location, the business faltered because Lewis had opened his doors without having the necessary funds behind him. Robert Lewis, a pharmaceutical drug broker and family friend, stepped in along with John Harrison, a wine merchant from Bread Street, and together all three men were able to settle the store on firmer financial ground. So firm, in fact, that a second shop was opened in George Yard, by Tower Hill, where Sir Walter Raleigh, who helped to popularize pipe smoking, had lost his head.*

* Raleigh's pipe pouch is inscribed: 'It was my companion in that most wretched time.'

In the early 1800s John Harrison's son, John Harrison III, wished to move the business to Great Newport Street, but Christopher Lewis resisted and when he retired his own son, Thomas Lewis, lacked the will to battle against Harrison's plans and so left the business in ill-will. Harrison then made his move, accompanied by Robert Lewis, who, after twenty-five years as a drug broker, changed his title on the books to that of 'merchant'.

The Great Newport Street shop was among the first in Britain to stock cigars, where Harrison added them to the array of tobaccos, snuffs, pipes and pouches and watched as the city's gentlemen became quietly obsessed. This tobacco wrapped in leaves had first arrived in the country in the knapsacks of the veterans of Wellington's army which had fought against the French forces during the Peninsular War in Spain, where cigars were passionately popular. Cigars altered the atmosphere in the shop. Where previously customers would collect their tobacco and promptly leave, now many were settling down on a tobacco tub to smoke and sip on an offered sherry. In 1830 John Harrison III moved the business to 10 Castle Street in Leicester Square where he was joined by his son, John Newman Harrison, who possessed a keen eye for property. Four years later, in

1834, the son acquired the lease on 81 St James's Street and, unable to find a tenant, he persuaded his father to open a second shop on the premises. Due to the success of St James's Street, the Castle Street business was closed down when John Harrison III retired.

John Newman Harrison's next innovation was to bring into the business the Robert Lewis whose name still hangs over the door today. Surprisingly little is known of this Robert Joseph Lewis, who is thought to have been a relative of the Robert Lewis who was the financial saviour of Christopher Lewis, the store's initial founder. What is known, however, is that he was a coffee broker who brought a hospitality to the trade that resulted in a glittering clientele and the shop's first royal warrant from the Duke of Edinburgh, a naval officer, who was the fourth child of Queen Victoria. The Duke's daughter Marie, the Queen of Romania, also became a client, as did Oscar Wilde, whose cigarettes were individually inscribed 'Oscar' in red letters.

The royal connection extended to the land on which the shop sat. A new lease was granted on 29 September 1873 on behalf of 'Her Majesty, The Queen, the Grand landlady', a description sure to leave Victoria far from amused should it have reached her ears. The lease lists 36 professions that the store was prohibited from practising, including 'vintner, distiller, tripe boiler, tallow melter and sugar baker'. Queen Victoria detested smoking as much as her husband, Albert, enjoyed it. Only the smoking room in the royal apartment was not marked with a 'V&A', instead being graced with a solitary 'A'.

The first European cigar aficionado is generally considered to be Rodriguo de Jerez, who began to smoke a daily cigar on 28 October 1492. The precise date was recorded seven days later in the logbook of Vincent Pinzon, captain of one of the three caravels on the first expedition made by Christopher Columbus to the New World. However, the date, is as suspect as (to contemporary eyes) were the 'cigars'. Columbus and his men only arrived in Cuba on 28 October 1492, twelve days after first breaking land in San Salvador. What is known is that de Jerez accompanied Luis de Torres, a Spanish translator fluent in Hebrew, Chaldean and Arabic, who explored the east of the island, spent time among the natives and recorded their smoking practices. Torres wrote: 'They carry a lighted piece of coal and some of the grasses, and inhale the aroma using catapults which in their language they call tobaccos.'

In Cuba the Indians used a Y-shaped hollow tube which they pushed amongst burning tobacco leaves before inhaling. Over the next twelve years Columbus and his crew would encounter a range of different tobacco practices as, during his four voyages, he explored Haiti, Guadeloupe, Puerto Rico, Jamaica, Venezuela, Colombia and Honduras. Yet others such as Ramon Pane, a monk who accompanied Columbus on his second voyage, laid claim to discovering the weed. Alvarez Pedro Cabral, a Portuguese explorer, is another name rolled into the discovery of tobacco. In 1500 he first landed in Brazil where all levels of society, men and women, smoked pipes and what resembled crude cigars, tobacco wrapped in different plant leaves.

Any cigar smoker who has glimpsed the divine through a haze of blue smoke will appreciate the practice's origin as a religious ceremony. In South America rudimentary cigars consisted of cured strips of tobacco wrapped in musa leaves or corn husks, which could reach a prodigious size of a metre or more, especially when rolled by shamans. Tribesmen would whittle special wooden supports shaped like tuning forks which could then be held in the hand or wedged in the ground.

On occasion carana granules were added to the cigars as they affected the smoker's vocal chords, giving them a deeper inflection which was considered more appropriate for communicating with the gods. The cigar smoke was used for healing, blessing and the nourishment of their spirit among Mayan, Incan and Aztec civilizations.

The very word 'cigar' is derived from the Mayans. The Quiche tribe used the term *jig* or *ciq* to describe their primitive cigars; this evolved into Ciq-Sigan, a term used by the Mayans, which evolved once again when wrapped around Spanish tongues. 'Cigales' first appeared in 1700 in the writings of Father Labat, a Dominican missionary who worked in the West Indies, while 'seegar' appeared in the *New English Dictionary* in 1735.

If Cuba first gave the Western world a glimpse of tobacco and the Mayans of South America lent the name, the actual birth of the modern cigar was in Spain. Tobacco first arrived in Europe in the sixteenth century. Cortez was said to have laid it at the feet of King Charles V of Spain in 1518, while Hernandez de Tuledo of Portugal, landed a cargo of leaves on the banks of the Tagus in 1520. In France Jean Nicot, the ambassador to Portugal made a present of plants to the Cardinal of

Lorraine in 1560 and of his name to nicotine. Once established, the taking of tobacco began in a medicinal manner, subsequently as a social pleasure first as snuff, then smoked in pipes.

In the seventeenth century there was a brief backlash against its use. King James I dismissed it as 'stinking grass' in 1619, and across Europe monarchs who had previously encouraged its use now penalized the practice. In Europe there was confiscation; in the Middle East amputation, with smokers suffering the loss of their lips and nose, but hostility to smoking was unsustainable in the face of its potential profit to the coffers of kings. Taxation was soon favoured over proscription, Queen Elizabeth I ordering a tax of twopence on each pound of tobacco arriving from the colonies of Virginia, a practice repeated by monarchs across the Continent.

In Spain the funds from taxation allowed the government to built factories in which the raw tobacco arriving from Cuba, now settled and firmly under Iberia's lash, was processed and then transformed into modern cigars, the first of which appeared in 1676. Spain's success was to find methods of curing and fermentation that led to the development of a tobacco leaf which could provide the wrapper – or outer envelope –

of the modern cigar. Previously this role was played by the leaves from other plants. In 1731 the royal factory in Seville, the Real Fabrica del Tabacos, was founded, and by 1800 5,000 people worked full-time in the production of the *puro* as the Spanish cigar was then called. Georges Bizet's opera *Carmen*, written in 1820, was inspired by the women who worked in the tobacco factories of Seville.

The machismo that continues to surround cigar smokers is tied to the Bandolero, the Spanish tobacco smugglers of the early nineteenth century. These rugged men favoured large moustaches, slung cartridge belts over their shoulders and wore full-length capes while riding semi-wild Andalusian stallions. The Bandoleros scorned both cold and hunger, insisting that all they required was 'wine, women, poetry and tobacco'. The most famous of their number were *los siete niños de Ecijoa* or 'the seven sons of Ecijoa', who won fame for stealing a consignment of cigars sent from Cuba to King Fernando VII. When the French invaded Spain in 1808 the Bandoleros joined forces with the British army, led by Sir Arthur Wellesley (later Duke of Wellington), and introduced the troops to the pleasures of cigars, which were easier than pipes to smoke on the march.

For nearly 150 years Spain had dominated the cigar

market and introduced cigars to other nations, but in 1817 the glow from this golden age began to dim. This was caused by the stroke of a pen when the Decreto Real was signed, an agreement that relaxed the monopoly under which all Cuban tobacco had but one destination: Spain. The beginning of the nineteenth century had been a time of farewells to the Spanish empire; she lost the silver mines of Peru, and Mexico broke free taking Florida and California with her. All that remained was Cuba and in an attempt to prevent the country from also snapping the bonds, Spain let out the leash. Cuba was now free to open to whomever she chose.

For many years there had been a black market in tobacco between Cuba and the United States. American citizens had developed a taste for cigars courtesy of General 'Abe' Putnam, who in 1762 had participated with British troops in the sack of Havana and claimed as many cigars as three donkeys could carry. He then sold them singly to customers at the tavern he owned in Connecticut. In time Connecticut imported tobacco seeds from Cuba and set up its own factory in 1810. The Decreto Real now allowed legitimate business to pass between the two countries, triggering a boom in sales. Yet this was not just America. It was soon discovered that cigars rolled in Cuba, then dispatched to Europe, retained their flavour and smoked far finer than those rolled using the same tobacco in Spain.

Seven years before the Decreto Real was introduced, the first trademark cigar had been registered in Havana: it was the name of Bernard Rencureel's, followed shortly by H. de. Cabanas y Carbjel. The nineteenth century saw the birth of the great cigar brands of today as dozens of new factories sprang up in Havana. In 1827 Partagas was founded; 1834 Por Larranaga; 1837 Ramon Allones; 1840 Punch; 1844 H. Upmann; 1848 El Rey del Mundo; 1865 Hoyo de Monterrey and in 1875 Romeo y Julieta. The birth of the twentieth century also brought forth Bolivar in 1902.

Romeo y Julieta, which would become a particular favourite of Winston Churchill, was founded by Inocensio Alvarez and Manin Garcia who set up a factory at Calle O'Reilly, which was within range of the cannon of the fort by the port of Havana. Both men could watch from their window as sailboats and the steamships (which were revolutionizing global trade) departed laden with cargoes of cigars. By 1845 tobacco had replaced sugar as the island's principal export, and by 1855 Cuba had 9,500 tobacco plantations, nearly 2,000 cigar manufacturers, and 150,000 people earned their living from the plant. Cuban cigars became celebrated around the world. The H. Upmann brand won medals at festivals in London (1862), Paris (1865) and Moscow (1872).

From seed to cigar can take at least three years, and by 1850 Cuban manufacturers had the system perfected. The finest tobacco leaves were found to grow in the Vuelta Abajo, a small triangle of land that contains fine, rich soil with the consistency of talcum powder, and is located in the island's western province of Pinar del Rio. The rhythm of the year was unchanging. In September the tobacco seeds were sown in nurseries, then, after forty-five days, seedlings were moved to the fields from mid-October onwards. Tobacco leaves require the right supply of sunshine, temperature and moisture, and too much water is disastrous. In the seventeenth century Erioxil Panduca, an Indian planter, said: 'The gods have decreed that tobacco only needs water twice a month. Too much water robs it of its honey.' The plants take a further 40 days to mature, after which the first leaves are ready to be picked. The harvest would begin in December and end in March or early April.

Harvesting was a labour-intensive process, with each plant demanding to be visited several times to collect two or three leaves at a picking in layers from the bottom upwards. The level from which the leaves were picked from the plant would be reflected in the strength of the tobacco when smoked. The longer the sun's rays had been cast on the plant, the stronger the tobacco would be, with the strongest tobacco derived from the leaves at the top of the plant. At harvest as many as sixteen leaves were taken from a single plant, two or three from each of the plant's seven levels, with the leaves closest to the ground used as the mildest in the blends.

The leaves were then tied together into pairs and draped over wooden poles in sets of fifty inside what was called the *casa de tabaco* – the curing barn – where they slowly dried out. Once dried and subsequently fermented, the leaves were scrutinized by hand and divided into two dozen different categories depending on size, colour, texture and pliability. They were then sealed inside bales and stored in warehouses to age for several years. Only then, at the factories, would the blending take place. For it was discovered that tobacco leaves of different origin could be blended together to achieve a uniform balanced taste.

The hand rolling of the cigar was standardized by the latter half of the nineteenth century. Five types of tobacco, three in the filler made from leaves taken from different levels, were wrapped by a single pliant binder leaf which in turn was rolled inside a wrapper, a leaf chosen for its colour and appearance. The factories where this took place were small stone rooms redolent with the scent of fresh tobacco and populated with a hierarchy of staff. The strippers were usually women. Their job was to remove not their clothes but the central vein of each tobacco leaf, which they did from piles of leaves resting on their thighs. This is the genesis of the myth that cigars are rolled on the thighs of Cuban beauties. Prosper Merimée described the work in his novella, *Carmen*, which later formed the basis of Bizet's opera. The strippers were often older women and among the most intimidating workers, quick to abuse owners and colleagues alike.

The aristocracy of cigar makers were the rollers, of whom it was said that they required six years to become competent, ten years to be proficient and a lifetime to achieve mastery, although few had the skills to achieve such a grade. These men, and in later years women, could take a bundle of leaves and roll a dozen cigars in an hour, moving nimbly through the nine different stages and producing a finished product with a fine vitola – the term given to describe the balance between size, strength, shape and presentation.

Like boys before and since, Winston Churchill learned to smoke at school. Cigarettes were not on the curriculum at Harrow, his public school,* yet despite this smoking was still diligently practised by the boys. When news of his habit reached his mother, Lady Randolph wrote on 19 September 1890 to her son that it was a practice best postponed by a boy who was not yet fifteen: 'Darling Winston, I hope you will try & not smoke. If you only knew how foolish and silly you look doing it you wd give it up, at least for a few years. If you will give it up & work hard this term to pass yr preliminary I will get Papa to get you a gun & a pony.'

Animals and armaments were surprising bribes to persuade a young boy to lay down the weed, but it worked. Winston replied the next day already adept at the negotiated compromise. His mother suggested 'several years'; he agreed to considerably shorter suspension, writing: 'I will leave off smoking for six months because I think you are right.'

Winston Churchill adored his mother though she, while loving, had little time for him. In later life he wrote: 'She shone for me like the evening star. I loved her dearly – but at a distance.'

Jeanette Churchill, or Jennie as she was known, was

* His father considered him too stupid for Eton, the establishment that had educated seven previous generations of Churchills.

the daughter of Leonard Jerome, a New York financier whose family owned 25 per cent of the *New York Times* but whose pockets were not quite deep enough to make his daughter an attractive catch for an English aristo-crat on his uppers hoping to trade a grand old name for a New World fortune. Lord Randolph Henry Spencer Churchill was the third son of the seventh Duke and a descendant of John Churchill, the first Duke of Marl-borough, whose victory at the Battle of Blenheim in 1704 during the War of the Spanish Succession saved Britain and Europe from French domination. Even without a solid financial foundation, Jennie was still a catch. A great beauty with thick black hair and bewitching eyes, she was nineteen and accompanying her mother and sister on a tour of European society when she first met Lord Randolph in August 1873 on board HMS *Ariadne* at a regatta at Cowes, on the Isle of Wight.

The couple were engaged three days later, wed at the British Embassy in Paris on 15 April 1874 and seven months later Winston Spencer Churchill was born prematurely during a visit to Blenheim Palace, the ancestral home, on 30 November 1874.

The marriage between Jennie and Lord Randolph was not a happy one, with affairs and indiscretions on both sides. While she was distracted by society life and he by the great game of Victorian politics – he would eventually rise to become Chancellor of the Exchequer – young Winston was raised by his nanny, Mrs Everest, whom he called 'Woom'.

A strong and wilful child, Winston Churchill was sent to St George's boarding school at Ascot at the age of eight. The headmaster, a sadist, took pleasure in caning the boys until their backsides bled, but no one could break Winston. When he was flogged for breaking into the pantry to steal sugar, he took his revenge by kicking the headmaster's straw hat to pieces. After being moved to another school, this time in Brighton, he arrived at Harrow in 1888 where he performed woefully in any subject that failed to engage his interest, which was everything save English and history. He detested Latin and refused to learn a language, writing to his mother, who suggested he spend time with a French family: 'No family! No family! Uggh!'

It was at school that Winston endured his father's wrath as he twice failed the entrance exam to Sandhurst, the military college for officers. Lord Randolph had watched with interest as his son carefully manoeuvred his toy soldiers and became convinced that a military career was crucial to prevent his son from becoming a failure. However, any notion that he might follow in his father's footsteps and attend Oxford University was sunk by Winston's poor grades. At one point Lord Randolph even wrote a cruel letter in which he threatened to sever their relationship: 'If you cannot prevent yourself from leading the idle useless unprofitable life you have had during your schooldays & later months you will become a mere social wastrel, one of the hundreds of the public school failures.'

However, Winston Churchill succeeded in securing a place at Sandhurst on his third attempt; this was with the cavalry, which set the lowest academic standards of all the military forces. He left Harrow with one precious achievement from which a lifetime's earnings would flow: 'I got into my bones the essential structure of the ordinary British sentence which is a noble thing.'

At Sandhurst Churchill moved from cigarettes to the preferred smoke of a gentleman: the cigar. His father, however, objected to this progression; he was already sending his son boxes of quality cigarettes which Winston saved for 'after lessons' while he 'smoked commoner ones in the daytime'. So Winston was informed by his mother of Lord Randolph's disagreement. He subsequently replied to his father and explained that his mother had 'written to me to tell me that you do not like my smoking cigars. I will not do so anymore, I am not fond enough of them in having any difficulty in leaving them off.' Like the politician he would become, Winston's promise was surprisingly fluid, for one week later he said: 'I will take your advice about the cigars and I don't think I shall often smoke more than one or two a day – and very rarely that.' It was another promise he found difficult to keep.

The death of Lord Randolph on 24 January 1895 had been preceded by a period of erratic and disturbing behaviour as syphilis tightened its grip on his mind. Lady Randolph tried to ease his suffering by taking her husband on a cruise around Europe, but it was of little use. Before his death Winston had insisted on learning the truth of his father's illness, and refused to allow it to diminish his affection for him. However deeply he felt the loss, it finally cleared the path for Winston to join the Queen's Own Hussars, a cavalry regiment against which had Randolph had been set.

On 21 October 1895, Churchill, while lodging at the Bachelors' Club in London, wrote to his mother of his plans to visit Cuba. He was happy to report that 'the Cuban business is satisfactorily settled'. By this he meant that the War Office had given their consent for him to travel as a neutral observer and to report to the Intelligence department on the effects of a new bullet – particularly 'its penetration and striking distance' – which was being used by the Spanish authorities to put down the latest uprising. Churchill had other plans: 'I shall bring back a great many Havana cigars' to be 'laid down' in the cellars of 35 Great Cumberland Place, the family's London home.

After a visit to New York and long train journey to Key West, followed by a short crossing to Cuba, Churchill arrived at Havana harbour on 20 November. His bags were carried the short distance to the Gran Hotel Inglaterra, whose wrought-iron terrace looked out on the maple trees and greenery of the central square. Here, as he recorded in *My Early Life*, his autobiography, 'we smoked cigars and ate oranges'. The exact brand of cigars which he smoked at that time is not recorded; however, given his future admiration for Romeo & Julieta, it is not difficult to picture him puffing softly on the fruits of their great factory, just a few streets away.

War, cigars and an afternoon siesta were to become integral elements of Churchill's life, and in Cuba he embraced them all. For it was here that he was first fired on. The war, which he had actively sought out, was a rebellion against Spanish rule that had first begun in 1868 and simmered for ten years before the abolition of slavery in 1880 turned down the heat. However, in the early months of 1895, the rebel leaders behind the original insurrection, Maximo Gomez and José Marti, returned from exile in America to stir up the island once again. Spain was forced to send out a large expeditionary force of 200 officers and 7,000 men with the twin task of putting down the rebellion and instituting further reforms which they hoped would win over the populace.

Churchill and his travelling companion, Reggie Barnes, set out on 21 November and travelled across the country by train to meet the Spanish forces under the command of General Valdez, former director of the military school in Madrid. Fortunately the pair missed their connection to Sancti Spiritus by thirty minutes, for as it happened the train was fired on and the railway line bombed. When they finally arrived at their destination, Winston would dismiss it as 'a forsaken place, and in the most unhealthy state, smallpox and yellow fever are rife'. Once united with General Valdez, Churchill marched with his men to the village of Iquana, which was blockaded by the insurgents, with the goal of protecting the supply convoy. A band of 4,000 insurgents, under the command of Maximo Gomez, was discovered to be encamped a few miles east and on 30 November, Churchill's twenty-first birthday, a short battle ensued. As he wrote: 'For the first time I heard shots fired in anger and heard bullets strike flesh and whistle through the air.'

It is comical that his love of bathing almost got him killed the following day. As he wrote in a dispatch to the *Graphic*, a British newspaper: 'My companions and I persuaded a couple of officers on the staff to come with us and bathe in the river.' The water may have been 'delightful, being warm and clear', but it was also dangerous, as their aquatic exercises came under fire and they had to flee in the buff, grabbing their clothes as they ran.

A staunch colonial who believed firmly in the civilizing influence of European power, Churchill's experience under fire with Spanish soldiers nevertheless left him torn on the issue of Cuban independence. In his first dispatch from the island he wrote: 'The demand for independence is national and unanimous. The insurgents gain support continually. There is no doubt that they possess the sympathy of the entire population.' On the other hand he was dismissive of their wasteful and cruel techniques. 'They neither fight bravely nor use their weapons effectively,' he wrote the following year. His conclusion at the time was: '. . . though the Spanish administration is bad, a Cuban government would be worse, equally corrupt, more capricious and far less stable. Under such a government revolutions would be periodic, property insecure, equity unknown.'

Yet in a letter to his mother, of 7 January 1897, he cast doubt on his initial verdict: 'I reproach myself somewhat for having written a little uncandidly and for having perhaps done injustice to the insurgents.'

Two years later Winston Churchill would once again enter a war under the guise of a spectator and enjoy cigars under less convivial surroundings. Instead of a hotel terrace, he was to puff away in the darkness of a coal mine.

On 18 September 1899, he was approached by the *Daily Mail* to travel to South Africa to report on the war that had just broken out between Britain and the Dutch Boers of the Transvaal. He had left the army the previous autumn after taking part in the last great cavalry charge, which took place in the Battle of Omdurman, during which hundreds of dervishes were slaughtered, to his disgust. The prospect of action, on a handsome salary, attracted him greatly; but it was not the *Daily Mail* that secured his words but the *Morning Post*, which agreed to pay him £250 a month (£8,000 in today's money). The Boer War would make Winston Churchill's name around the world, though it was his capture and subsequent escape rather than any victory that made the telegraph wires hum.

On 15 November 1899, he set off onboard an armoured train under the command of Captain Aylmer Haldane, an old army friend. Unfortunately the train track was sabotaged, the train itself attacked, and despite Churchill's valiant attempt to save the engine, he was forced to surrender along with Haldane's men. Detained at the State Model School in Pretoria, he argued that as a journalist rather than an enlisted officer, he should be released, but this fell on deaf ears. Yet if the Boers would not provide his freedom, he would liberate himself. On the evening of 12 December Churchill, Haldane and another soldier planned to sneak over the fence. Only Winston succeeded, while the other two were detained by the changing of a guard. Churchill then embarked on an adventure straight from the pages of John Buchan.* In the role of Richard Hannay,

* See *The 39 Steps*.

he leapt aboard and stowed away on a train to Witbank, 75 miles from Pretoria. There he boldly knocked on the door of John Howard, manager of the Transvaal and Delgao Bay Colliery. Since Howard was British, this was one of the only safe houses for 20 miles. Howard's solution was to stow him down a mine shaft for two days, but he ensured he was accompanied by creature comforts: 'Mr Howard handed me a couple of candles, and a bottle of whisky and a box of cigars.'

After emerging from the stygian gloom, Churchill was loaded (hidden in bales of wool) onto a train bound for Portuguese East Africa. He was accompanied by Charles Burnham, a local storekeeper, who kept inquisitive soldiers and the local sheriff at bay until the train was across the border. At Ressano Garcia, the first stop in Portuguese territory, Churchill emerged and fired his pistol in celebration.

When Winston Churchill stepped into Robert Lewis on that warm August day in 1900, he was already a war veteran, a celebrated journalist, acclaimed author and now on the brink of a new political career. In 1899 he had stood as the Conservative candidate for Oldham and lost. In the autumn of 1900, as the leaves turned brown and fell, a general election was called and, once again, Churchill stood for the constituency of Oldham. This time he won.

The cigar on which he puffed after the results had been called in his favour was sweet. He was entering the smoke-filled rooms of politics and power. Now Winston Churchill, equipped with supplies from Robert Lewis, would provide his own smoke.

TWO

==

HUMIDOR AND HOME

'How can I tell that my temper would have been as sweet or my companionship as agreeable if I had abjured from my youth the goddess Nicotine?

Winston Churchill in an essay,
'A Second Choice'.

O N THE CHILL morning of 26 December 1926, the four children of Winston Churchill and his wife Clementine ran gaily through the corridors of Chartwell, the sixteenth-century manor house that had become the family home. It was four years since the morning in mid-September when he had loaded his three eldest children – Diana, then 13, Randolph, 11, and Sarah, 7 – into the old Wolseley car and departed the din of London for the quiet of the Kent countryside. After less than an hour's drive they reached the imposing brown brick house under whose timber beams Henry VIII had once slept while courting Anne Boleyn. 'Do you like it?' Churchill asked his 'kittens', as he referred to them in letters to Clemmie. The response was a chorus of: 'Do buy it! Do buy it!' In fact, he had already done so.

Clementine's response was less enthusiastic. She had wished for a 'little country basket', where they could relax as a family; instead Churchill had plumped for a giant battered steamer trunk, in need of considerable renovation that would cost almost four times the £5,000 purchase price, take just under two years to complete and try the patience and fray the nerves of Philip Tilden, the architect charged with the task. For as he wrote: 'No client that I ever had, considering his well-filled life, has ever spent more time, trouble, or interest in the making of his home than did Mr Churchill.'

Now racing from the library, wallpapered with books on politics and war and not a few of their father's own, the children sped on through their mother's sitting room, past the drawing room and downstairs to the dining room. The object of the exercise was to gather up as many bottles of champagne and vintage wine (empty, of course) as they could. Christmas was the family's favourite time of year. As Mary would later recall: 'When we were all assembled on Christmas Eve, the double doors between the drawing room and the library were flung open to reveal the Christmas tree, glowing with light, and radiating warmth, and a piny, waxy smell from a hundred real white wax candles.'

The purpose of gathering up the detritus of a wonderful Christmas Day was in order to imprint the memory in paint. Churchill had a mind to compose a new still life and so, as the children watched, he positioned myriad coloured bottles on the dining-room cabinet. But something was missing. The solution, as so often the casel in life, came in a couple of cigar boxes which were soon nestled among the forest of bottles. Behind the easel, in painter's white smock and with a cigar between his lips, Churchill set to work over the next few hours creating 'Bottlescape' as the completed work would be called. It was only fitting that he include the cigar boxes, for Chartwell was not just his home but in time his humidor.

The cigars, which one day would rise in number to around 3,000, were stored in a tiny room on the first floor, between his bedchamber and study. There they sat in boxes on shelves labelled 'wrapped', 'naked' and 'large'. Although friends often presented him with cigar cutters, he never used them. On 30 November 1913, his mother gave him a solid silver cigar cutter for his thirty-ninth birthday; though treasured, as any act of affection from his mother always was, it too was never utilized. Instead Churchill had two systems for preparing cigars.

He would either make a small V-shaped cut on the head or use a large match to pierce the cigar, then blow through it from the other end in order to clear a passage. The cigars were lit using a candle that sat on the stand by his bed, or with long-stem matches. He also had a unique system for coping with frayed or soggy cigars by simply using gummed brown paper to wrap the end in a paper girdle which he called a 'bellyband'.

The cigar was commonly smoked by politicians in the Edwardian era, though no one used it so effectively as prop and physical tool as Winston Churchill. It was the object's sheer ubiquity, the fact that he was literally never seen without one, that succeeded in fusing Churchill and his cigar into the public's imagination as one inseparable item. He was also aware of the image the cigar projected, one of relaxed confidence, and the appeal this would have with the electorate. It was likewise a weathervane to his stormy moods since it could be casually removed from his mouth and waved in the air to make a mild point or, if he was particularly enraged, an order or command would be barked with the cigar still wedged between his teeth. At a political meeting he would use it as an effective distraction from a speaker with whom he disagreed. Churchill would make great play of preparing the cigar, striking the

match repeatedly and then puffing away, at times pro-
voking the speaker to pause until the commotion had
passed. At more private gatherings, round the Cabinet
table for instance, he would quietly smoke and allow the
ash to build up around the tip until it formed half
the length of the cigar. Colleagues would become spell-
bound as it appeared to defy gravity and would become
distracted from the speaker as they waited for the ash
to drop, unaware that Churchill had pierced the cigar
with a long pin around which the ash now clung.

Churchill was also aware of the benefit and ease that
smoking a cigar would bring to his mind. He wrote, in
an essay called 'A Second Choice':

I remember my father in his most sparkling mood,
his eye gleaming through the haze of a cigarette,
saying, 'Why begin? If you want to have an eye that
is true (and) a hand that does not quiver . . . don't
smoke.' But consider! How can I tell that the soothing influence of tobacco upon my nervous system
may not have enabled me to comport myself with
calm and courtesy in some awkward personal
encounter or negotiation, or carried me serenely
through some critical hours of anxious waiting?
How can I tell that my temper would have been as

41

sweet or my companionship as agreeable if I had not abjured from my youth the goddess Nicotine?

Standing, quietly painting 'Bottlescape' while puffing softly on his cigar, if Churchill had reflected on his life so far, what would he have found? At that very moment in 1926 he stood at the peak of his political career to date. Since November 1924, he had been Chancellor of the Exchequer, the second highest political post, next door both figuratively and literally to the Prime Minister, then Stanley Baldwin. Managing the nation's budget, guarding her purse strings, did not come naturally to a man who was so loose with his own. However, he did succeed in pinching pennies by refusing to fund a military base in Singapore, stating: 'For what? A war with the Japanese.' His decision to reintroduce the gold standard led to the over-valuation of the pound, which was later viewed as a disastrous mistake. Yet after a career that had already wound through both dark valley and sunny uplands, he was content to be following in his father's footsteps; in fact, he wore Lord Randolph's robes of office.

In the final scene of *Young Winston* (1972), Richard

Attenborough's film of his early life, Simon Ward as Winston is seen lifting a cigar to his lips after his maiden speech in the House of Commons on 18 February 1901. His mother steps forward to light it, in a potent symbol of his passage into manhood.

Although elected as a member of the Conservative Party, Churchill viewed himself as an old Tory, in his father's mould. He saw the role of government as not simply to prop up the landed classes, but to provide more pastoral care to the working class too. His passionate belief in free trade, as opposed to the Conservative Government's policy of tariffs on imports and exemptions for colonial countries, prompted him to join the 'Hughligans' or 'Hooligans', a loose collection of Tory dissidents led by Lord Hugh Cecil. In 1904 he chose to 'cross the floor' and sit with the Liberals, which was to earn him the lasting enmity of the Conservative Party, but more immediately it earned him the office of Under Secretary of Colonial Affairs. In this role he undertook a tour of Africa, wrote a book on his experiences and granted self-governance to the Transvaal and the Orange Free State. By 1905 he had also completed a two-volume biography of Lord Randolph Churchill, which went some distance to repairing his father's tattered reputation.

The happiest period of his life began in 1908. The Prime Minister, Herbert Asquith, appointed him to the Cabinet as President of the Board of Trade, where he advocated shorter working hours, educational opportunities and the creation of employment agencies. Most importantly, he married the lady who truly was the love of his life.

Winston first met Clementine Hozier in 1904, but it was not until she visited his mother's house in April 1908 that she captured his heart. By all accounts, she was poor but of good (if unreliable) breeding. Her mother, Blanche, the daughter of an earl, had struggled to ensure a respectable upbringing for her three daughters after her husband, Colonel Sir Henry Hozier, abandoned them. Clementine was blessed with good sense, a keen mind, charm and great beauty; but most importantly to Churchill, she had character. On the morning of 11 August the couple visited Blenheim Palace and, at the temple of Diana, he proposed and she accepted. The couple wed less than one month later, on 12 September 1908.

Churchill went on to become Home Secretary where he, undeservedly, earned the reputation of being hostile to the working class. This was on account of his handling of the riots in the Welsh town of Tonypandy, where he was forced to deploy both police and army against striking miners. The public did not see the long hours he spent poring over the trials of the condemned, advocating their case to his conscience and often awarding, where possible, clemency from the gallows. Yet the image of Churchill as hard and unsympathetic was only compounded by his appearance at the scene of the Sydney Street siege, in the East End of London, where three anarchists were holed up following the murder of a policeman. A photographer caught him, dressed in top hat and astrakhan coat, directing the troops.

Leadership from the front was a policy he continued on his appointment as First Lord of the Admiralty in October 1911. The rise in German sea power had been a cause of concern, and while Home Secretary he had been familiar with the worrying reports compiled by the Secret Service Bureau, forerunner of MI5 and MI6. Shortly after assuming the new role he caused controversy by stating publicly that for Britain a large navy was a 'necessity', but was a 'luxury' for Germany. He prepared with diligence and vigour for the coming war; the fleet was converted from coal to oil engines, and to ensure a steady supply of fuel he bought 51 per cent of the Anglo-Iran Oil Company. When the Government wavered over the construction of more ships, he threatened resignation and won his way. When war finally broke out in September 1914, he confessed his state of mind in a letter to Clementine: 'Everything tends towards catastrophe and collapse. I am interested, geared up and happy. Is it not terrible to be built like that?'

And yet, for all his enthusiasm, Churchill had a disastrous war. Where, prior to 1914, the cry against him was 'remember Tonypandy', afterwards it would become 'remember Gallipoli'. The decision, on 18 March 1915, to launch an attack on the Gallipoli peninsula as a means of defeating the Turks and allowing safe passage through the Dardanelles to supply the Russians in the Black Sea, was a plan Churchill had pioneered, but it was carried out in a manner which he did not. Instead of a combined naval and infantry assault, the navy steamed in first but then withdrew after the loss of three ships. Troops then followed unsupported, only to be pinned down in what became the slow, tortuous grind of trench warfare which would eventually lead to the deaths of 46,000 allied soldiers.

Admiral Sir John Fisher, then First Sea Lord, who had helped to plan the attack and who previously signed his letters to Churchill, 'Yours until Hell freezes over', ran off like melting snow and went to ground as

Winston struggled for his political life. Offered the post of Chancellor of the Duchy of Lancaster, a non-Cabinet position, Churchill was devastated, writing that he felt: '. . . like a sea beast fished up from the depths or a diver too suddenly hoisted, my veins threatened to burst from the fall in pressure.'

The depression into which Churchill sank led to the discovery of a pastime which, like oil to canvas, was a balm to his spirits. In the summer of 1915 the family had rented Hoe Farm, a house near Godalming in Surrey where they retired at weekends, joined where possible by Churchill's brother Jack and sister-in-law Goonie. In the garden one summer morning, he came upon Goonie painting. She noted his interest and equipped him with a spare canvas and some watercolours, which he quickly switched for oils as he embarked on yet another career to add to those of soldier, politician and writer. He would become a painter as well, completing over 500 canvases and later enjoying a one-man show at the Diploma Gallery of the Royal Academy in 1959.

The paintbrush was like a stick thrown to the Black Dog of depression, one which sent it sullenly stalking off. As his secretary, Edward Marsh, said: '[it was] a distraction and a sedative that brought a measure of ease to his frustrated spirit.' War, or more accurately the command of men, would prove a similar sedative. For in the autumn of 1915, Churchill resigned from government and travelled to France to, eventually, take command of the 6th Royal Scots Fusiliers. Dressed rather oddly in a French steel helmet, he won the respect and affection of his men during his six months in trench mud. He may not have shared out the 'Stilton, cream, hams, sardine, a big beefsteak pie' that he instructed Clementine to dispatch, but he did share the dangers by inspecting the trenches several times each day. He was also generous with his cigars and so fate was generous with him, for he benefited from a window of calm on the Western Front. He arrived too late for the Battle of Loos and departed too early for the Battle of the Somme. War, for him, had been a tonic: 'I have found happiness and content such as I have not known for many months.'

Churchill returned to government in July 1917. Prime Minister Herbert Asquith, whom he had mocked as 'supine, sodden and supreme', had been replaced by Lloyd George, who appointed him as Minister for Munitions, in which role – accompanied by a bust of

Napoleon – he compressed departments, prevented strikes and solved grievances. The end of the war in November 1918 rather took him by surprise, but his star was back in the ascendant as he was promoted to Secretary for War and Air, later becoming Colonial Secretary in 1921. In this latter role he negotiated the Anglo-Irish treaty that partitioned the country between the Unionist north and the nationalist south and on which Michael Collins, the IRA leader, declared: 'Tell Winston we couldn't have done anything without him.' From Ireland his remit roamed to the Middle East, where he was responsible for ensuring that Emir Faisal should become the King of Iraq, though that country would in essence be run by Britain. Yet 1921 would be a year remembered most bitterly for personal strife and three tragic deaths. First Clementine's brother, Bill, committed suicide in a Paris hotel room; then Winston's beloved mother, Lady Randolph, died after tripping in high heels and falling downstairs; and finally, and most tragically, the couple's daughter Marigold died of a diphtheria-like illness when aged just three. Churchill wrote: 'What changes in a year, what gaps, what a sense of fleeting shadows.'

The following year brought professional disappointment when Lloyd George's Government collapsed and, recovering from an operation to remove his appendix,

Churchill failed to retain his seat in Dundee despite the sterling efforts of his wife, who campaigned on his behalf. 'I found myself without an office, without a seat, without a party and without an appendix,' he later wrote.

Work, as it always would, brought solace and income, and he used the free time to complete his history of the First World War, *The World Crisis*, before returning to Parliament, this time as the Conservative MP for Epping in October 1924, and shortly afterwards to government as Chancellor.

The production of memos, letters, books and hundreds of newspaper articles meant that Churchill's study at Chartwell had become the engine room of a powerful machine whose later purpose was to awaken the British nation and her government to the reality of Nazi aggression. He called it 'the factory'. The act of smoking was inextricably linked to that of writing. Dictation was carried out as he paced the room and puffed on a cigar. Proofs were corrected and inadvertently scattered with ash. Cigars were an aid to both meditation and composition as Commander Thompson, his personal bodyguard, recalled: 'He did not inhale the smoke, but blew it about in meditative balloons, often peering into them as if they were fish pools, or as if he might have dropped something of value into their centre and were seeking to locate it.'

At Robert Lewis, on St James's Street, there had recently been a change of guard. When Winston Churchill first visited the shop in August 1900, Frederick George Croley was a nineteen-year-old boy, just two years in the trade and not suitably attired to work on the front counter and serve 'gentlemen'. The second son of a manufacturer of ladies' mantles and a Buckingham blacksmith's daughter, Fred had joined Robert Lewis as a sixteen-year-old 'dogsbody'. He was so poorly paid that he walked to Brixton and back rather than spend a penny each way on the horse-drawn tram. He was as thrifty as José Pinto, who bought the business shortly after his arrival, was profligate, yet over the next forty-five years the pair became close friends.

Fred graduated from his early task of meeting Mr Pinto's cab each morning, and carting out his monstrously fat cat, to developing the mail-order business. When Mr Pinto travelled across England securing orders from regional tobacconists he invariably took Fred and the pair would take rooms in the finer hotels where the Havanas would be laid out. Fred met his wife on these road trips: Lilly Bennett, the daughter of a stationmaster at Penzance, worked for a tobacconist to whom he sold cigars. They had three children – Joan, John and Ruth. In January 1918 Fred Croley was made partner in the business and was so successful with the development of the wholesale side that they moved premises from Bloomsbury to Grosvenor Square.

To commemorate the first anniversary of the partnership Pinto presented Croley with a gold pocket watch as a 'very inadequate token of my appreciation and sincere affection'. He had greater need to thank Croley in the mid-1920s when the retail manager of the St James's Street store resigned and the discovery was made that the business was in financial straits. However, by ruthless pruning and meticulous efficiency Croley corrected the company's course and reached calmer waters and a shallow profitability. Churchill would have been unaware how valued his custom had been, especially given his preference for credit and tardiness in settling any financial accounts.

During this period Churchill was not only purchasing cigars from five different London cigar suppliers, he also frequented the cigar store at Dunhill, the luxury goods shop on Duke Street in the heart of St James's, which was situated opposite the Turkish baths – popular with the Prince of Wales, who would often pop in for a smoke after a steam. Like Robert Lewis, which was just around the corner, Dunhill had a commissionaire, a former officer in the Royal Horse Guards, and also tipped the cabbies who deposited customers with ten cigarettes from a discontinued line which had been produced for soldiers during the Great War. The cigar room was in the basement, furnished in rich mahogany with a thick green carpet, and illuminated by Venetian glass lights. It remained under the watchful eye of Major Malcolm Somerset-Johnstone, an ex-Household Cavalry officer who favoured a silk hat and monocle, and retrieved the finest cigars from a huge mahogany cabinet that, according to rumour, came from the Duke of Devonshire's mansion in Piccadilly. As G.H.M. Dee recalled in his house memoir: 'The large cedar-lined chamber was flanked by massive cabinets of Havana cigars. Domestic or British-made "own brands" were also in evidence and of those I remember "Flor de Lorenz", "Flor del Punto".'

Then there was Henry Wilson & Sons of Pall Mall, 'importers of choice' cigars who, on 1 April 1935, had reserved 500 cigars for Churchill but pointed out: '. . . that 500 is considerably less than you would normally smoke within 12 months; a period which is very short in which to condition and mature tobacco of this type.' The fact that the proprietor believed he was solely responsible for providing Churchill's cigars strengthens the possibility that Winston liked each of his suppliers to believe that they possessed an exclusive contract for his cigar needs.

In July 1935 Churchill had problems with another supplier when the Pinar Del Rio Havana Cigar Company in Princes Square, Mayfair, sent a consignment of double coronas to Chartwell that were below par. As Churchill's secretary explained:

He is very much disappointed with the last boxes of cigars which you sent him. They did not seem to be as well matured as those previously sent to him and this consignment actually appears to be damp. Could you let him know what the reason of this is? Both places for keeping cigars at the country address and the London flat are exceptionally dry, and have been chosen for this very reason, as Mr Churchill is extremely particular regarding the condition of the cigars. Perhaps you will go into the matter and let Mr Churchill know in due course why that is.

The following day's post brought an apology and explanation from Richard Milbanke, a director of the Pinar Del Rio Havana Cigar Co., who said:

> The double coronas have lately been in such demand that, although we have plenty in our maturing room and in bond, they are not and will not be in perfect smoking condition for at least six weeks. We theretofore venture to suggest that if you will be so good as to return the boxes sent to Mr Churchill we will send in their place special coronas. These cigars cost 10/- per 100 more than the double coronas but we would of course make no extra charge in this connection. We need hardly say how much we value Mr Churchill's patronage and how extremely sorry we are that he should have received his cigars out of condition.

However, it was a patronage they seemed destined to lose, as the following year Churchill began to order instead from the Galata Cigarette Company, Havana cigar and cigarette merchants owned by Mr J. Zitelli, a Turkish businessman who opened the store in Carlton Street, near Piccadilly Circus, at the turn of the century. In July 1936 Churchill was sent a sample box containing

two cigars each of seven different brands: the El
Safos Hidalgo; Cabana Patriarcas; Romeo y Julieta
selection disinatilas no. 2; Lord Beaconsfield Diademas
Grandes; A. Allones Corona Imperial; Romeo Julieta
Corona Superbas; Calixto Lopez-Lucullus. The sample
box came to a total of £1. 10 shillings for the fourteen
cigars.

One week later, on 20 July 1936, Mr Zitelli sold three
more samples of smaller cigars and assured Churchill
of 'our personal and prompt attention'. Unfortunately
a later cabinet of La Flor de A Allones cigars were
returned as Churchill had found them 'rather too
closely bound'. Nonetheless, Winston was satisfied with
Zitelli's services and he was retained, with the store providing many of Churchill's Romeo y Julieta cigars as
well as Patriarcas.

However, there was one incident that threatened to
terminate their relationship when in August 1941 Mr
Zitelli was tricked by a wily newspaper reporter posing
as a customer into revealing the secrets of the Prime
Minister's cigar supply. Under a headline in the London
News Chronicle which read, 'Churchill's cigar supply
getting low', the story explained that despite the fall in
the supply of Cuban cigars, Churchill had refused to
hoard. Mr Zitelli was quoted as saying: 'Before going for

a holiday recently, I sent him 600. But he sent them back saying that he had no wish to become a hoarder.' Instead it was explained that Churchill bought his cigars in bundles of 25 at a time. Mr Zitelli also revealed that, while not smoking the most expensive brands, Churchill was still the finest judge of cigars he had ever met. The article ended: 'Mr Zitelli says that no one who can select a fine cigar with the unerring instinct of Winston Churchill "can possibly be anything but a very great gentleman."' A forgiving gentleman too.

After publication Zitelli immediately wrote to Mrs Hill, Churchill's private secretary, to explain:

> I feel it is my duty to inform you that I gave no interview to the journalist who composed this enclosed article, nor have I given my consent or permission for the story to be printed in the *News Chronicle*. In fact I was not aware I was talking to a pressman when he called here to purchase some cigars in the usual way. I very much regret if inadvertently I may have caused any annoyance or inconvenience to our great Prime Minister.

The letter is marked: 'Telephoned message of thanks,

and told him that the Prime Minister had said he was not to worry about the matter. K.H.'

The effect of Winston Churchill's incessant cigar smoking on his health appears at first glance to be negligible, considering the fact that he died at the age of 90. Cigarette smoking was viewed as dangerous by Churchill, but not the cigar. He once admonished his valet, Frank Sawyer, who refused a cigar in favour of a cigarette, 'Too many of those will kill you.' Randolph Churchill, his son and a relentless chain-smoker who could inhale 80 to 100 cigarettes in a day, was severely criticized by his father for his habit. During the Second World War he wrote to Randolph:

> I had a hope that the difficulties of your commissariat would enforce abstention from the endless cigarette. If you can get rid of your husky voice and get back the timbre which your aged father still possesses, it might affect the whole future of your political career. It may be that abandoning cigarettes may not be the remedy, but it is in my bones that it is worth trying. Your sisters told me that it

was in the Liverpool election that with a very sore
throat and against doctor's warnings, you bellowed
for a considerable time in the market place. Weigh
these counsels of a friend, even if you are unwilling
to receive them from a father.

Yet Churchill was also asked to cut down his cigars on
medical advice. In August 1936 he complained to Dr
Thomas Hunt that he was suffering from painful indigestion, which he believed had been brought on by too
much mental exertion. It had been a tough year in
which the pendulum had only just begun to swing in his
direction. Following the German invasion of the
Rhineland in March, he had been invited to join a cross-
party pressure group set up to examine Britain's armed
forces.

In order to treat the indigestion he was asked to
avoid highly seasoned food such as 'cooked cheeses,
high game, strong coffee etc'. A specific medicinal
powder was to be taken twice a day and, wrote Dr Hunt:
'Cigars: to use a holder and reduce the number.' The
image of Churchill fitting his exceedingly long cigars
into a holder which would extend them even further
from his face is comical. During the war, he was asked
again by Lord Moran to reduce the number of cigars

he smoked, while on 18 December 1953 he was attacked by his own matchbox. As Lord Moran recorded in his diaries: 'The P.M. had been lunching at Trinity House, where Anthony [Eden] was elected [to the] Elder Brethren, when he put down his cigar on his plate so that a box of matches burst into flames. He had some big blisters on his left hand.'

The question of how many cigars Churchill actually smoked each day is difficult to answer: it could quite easily be as few as three or as many as ten, for although he was rarely without a cigar between his fingers or lips, it was not always lit. His bodyguard, Commander Thompson, wrote in his autobiography:

> It is true Churchill usually has a cigar in his mouth, but if you remember the motion pictures of him, you will recall that he does not seem to be smoking the cigar. And this is true. He will light a cigar immediately after breakfast, having been relighted innumerable times and quite as often abandoned soon after. He chews cigars, he doesn't smoke them. And his average of cigars destroyed is five per day.

Thompson also estimated that Winston re-lit his cigar an average of seven times. Yet it would be wrong to conclude from the detective's quotation that Churchill did not smoke. The testimony of his secretaries, who took dictation or typed among the cloudy billows, will pour cold water over such an idea. As Elizabeth Nel wrote in *Mr Churchill's Secretary*: 'Sometimes he would pause to light a cigar, which with so much concentration was neglected and frequently went out.'

Nevertheless, Churchill could be cagey about his own smoking habits. On a train journey he once asked Lord Cherwell, a brilliant mathematician, to calculate how much champagne he had consumed, at a rate of one pint per day, during his lifetime. Churchill was impressed with the final figure but disappointed that it could have been carried at one end of one railway coach. He had imagined an entire fleet would be pressed into service to drag the laden cargo. Yet when Cherwell suggested they calculate how many yards of cigars he had smoked, the Prime Minister, strangely, '. . . wouldn't go into it.'

From behind the easel at Chartwell on Boxing Day 1926, Churchill could not yet see the Dark Valley into which he, and the rest of the world, would fall during the

1930s. As Chancellor he remained near the summit, but not for much longer. In 1929 the Conservative Government was defeated by Labour and two years later Churchill chose to resign from what would now be called the Shadow Cabinet rather than support the party's position on greater independence for India. Instead he retreated to Chartwell to crank up the great wheels of industry which over the next decade would spin out his charming memoir, *My Early Life*, followed by the four-volume life of his ancestor, Marlborough, and hundreds of newspaper articles – delivered by his chauffeur, with instructions to wait for the cheque. The reason for such productivity was to cover the losses he had sustained in the Wall Street Crash of 1929 and to maintain a lifestyle that continued to include, as John Keegan, the military historian, wrote: 'Cruises, foreign holidays, opulent motor cars, dinners, grand hotels, squads of secretaries and servants, the best schools for his children, silk underwear and Havana cigars for himself.'

The 1930s saw the rise of totalitarian politics in Europe and the Far East. Mussolini had opened the gate in 1922 when he overthrew the Italian Liberal Government and, for a few years, he was the Continent's darling. Churchill went on to describe him as 'the greatest lawgiver among living men'. Japan then followed and, most disastrously, there was Germany, where Adolf Hitler secured power in January 1933. Churchill was researching his multi-volume biography in Germany when a friend offered to introduce him to the nation's new Chancellor. The opportunity of what would have been a historic encounter dissipated when Hitler heard of Churchill's mockery of the Nazi Party's anti-Jewish policies. One month after Hitler's ascent to power, Churchill gave a speech at Oxford, where he said: 'I think of Germany with its splendid clear-eyed youth marching forward on all the roads of the Reich, singing their ancient songs, demanding to be conscripted into an army; eagerly seeking the most terrible weapons of war; burning to suffer and die for the Fatherland.'

In speeches from the back benches of the House of Commons and from the columns of the *Daily Express* and *Evening Standard*, Churchill would urge the Government to take note of Germany's new militarism, to challenge them now or at least to make adequate preparation for a future war. The Government under Neville Chamberlain was reluctant to face facts. Britain had undergone an economic collapse in 1931, 3 million were unemployed out of a working population of 20 million. Veterans of the Great War were joining hunger marches on London. The Government preferred to spend what money they had, not on new ships which they denied to the navy, or modern aircraft for the fledgling RAF, but on unemployment relief and export subsidies.

Meanwhile Hitler was saying 'Yes' to all that the Treaty of Versailles (1919) had previously said 'No': such as an air force, an expansive navy, heavy artillery and tanks. In October 1934 he ordered the construction of a new fleet of tanks; in March 1935 he created an air force and reintroduced conscription. At a time when the German army was smaller than those of Poland and Czechoslovakia, nevertheless Hitler managed to bully Britain to agree to the construction of submarines in 1936. The British Government still believed that re-armament would be destructive to the nation's fragile economic reawakening, but Churchill's persistent lobbying did have some results. In 1932 the Government agreed to drop the 'ten-year-rule' – a policy of not expecting, nor preparing for, any armed conflict during this period. His speeches to the House of Commons were given added weight by the secret papers smuggled to him by civil servants who could see the dangers ahead even if their political masters refused to look.

In 1937 the aggression that Hitler had originally directed internally towards the Jewish people and gyp-

sies, the socialists and opponents of the regime was
exported towards Austria, Czechoslovakia and Poland.
On II March Hitler ordered his troops into Austria ahead
of the results of a national plebiscite on integration with
Germany. When his eye then turned towards Czechoslovakia, Churchill implored Britain to join '. . . in a
solemn treaty for mutual defence against aggression'.
He continued:

> If it were done in the year 1938 – and believe me it
> may be the last chance there will be for doing it –
> then I say that you might even now arrest this
> approaching war . . . Let those who wish to reject it
> ponder well and earnestly upon what will happen
> to us, if when all else has been thrown to the wolves,
> we are left to face our fate alone.

This was exactly what followed. There would be no
confrontation in 1938, only Neville Chamberlain's
ignominious flight to Berchtesgaden, Hitler's mountain
retreat, the first of three meetings that would result in
the Munich Agreement, which handed the Sudetenland
to Germany and gave the British Prime Minister his
brief pretence of 'Peace in our Time'.

The Munich Agreement provoked one of Churchill's

greatest speeches when on 5 October he rose to his feet in the House of Commons and declared:

All is over. Silent, mournful, abandoned, broken Czechoslovakia recedes into the darkness . . . I have tried my best to urge the maintenance of every bulwark of defence – first the timely creation of a (superior) air force; secondly the gathering together of the collective strength of many nations; and thirdly, the making of alliances . . . It has all been in vain. Every position has been successively undermined and abandoned on specious and plausible excuse.

[He went on] I do not grudge our loyal and brave people the spontaneous outburst of joy and relief when they learned that the hard ordeal would no longer be required of them at the moment . . . But they should know the truth. They should know that there has been gross neglect and deficiency in our defences; they should know that we have sustained a defeat without war . . . They should know that we have passed an awful milestone in our history, when the equilibrium of Europe has been deranged . . . and do not suppose that this is the end. This is only the first sip, the first foretaste of a bitter cup which

will be proffered to us year by year unless by a
supreme recovery of moral health and martial
vigour, we arise again and take our stand for freedom as in the olden time.

Churchill's powerful oratory helped to galvanize thirty
Conservative MPs to abstain from voting on the Munich
debate, while Anthony Eden and Duff Cooper, ministers both, resigned in protest. Unsatisfied, on 15 March
1939, the wolves of the Third Reich moved on the
remainder of Czechoslovakia.

A line, which should have been drawn long before,
was finally drawn at Poland. The German invasion on
1 September 1939 brought Britain into a state of war
with Germany, and Churchill back into the Cabinet as,
once again, First Lord of the Admiralty, a position he
would hold for just eight months before succeeding
Chamberlain as Prime Minister. The message which
legend declares was sent to the fleet, though no sup-
porting evidence can be found, read: 'Winston is Back'.

On the eve of the outbreak of the Second World War
the German Air Attaché visited the cigar store at Dunhill and bought 1,000 'Partagas' cigars for Hermann
Goering. The head of the Luftwaffe was an Epicurean
who possessed as hearty an appetite for champagne,

fine wine, good food and hand-rolled cigars as Churchill. It is interesting to speculate if Goering was doing more than satisfying his own desire and was, in fact, already attempting to blockade his future foe. Goering obviously became a fan of Dunhill cigars; after the fall of France, he purchased fresh supplies at the company's shop on the rue de la Paix, although this did not stop his air force from bombing the London store in the early hours of 17 April 1941 with two parchuted land mines.

Yet Alfred Dunhill, the store's owner, would display the fighting spirit that infused the whole nation by setting up a simple table in the midst of the rubble where he sold cigars to passers-by.

THREE

PROTECTING THE
PRIME MINISTER

'It is impossible for me to test the cigars
for every known poison.'

Dr Gerald Roche Lynch

DR GERALD ROCHE LYNCH stared at the mouse which did not stare back, for at that moment in late September 1941 the mouse was quite dead.

The death of a mouse while in the custody of the man known as the 'king's poisoner' was scarcely a surprise, but when the small mammal had recently ingested a broth whose principal ingredient was tobacco flakes from one of Winston Churchill's cigars, the mouse's demise was quite possibly a matter of the gravest national security.

The director of the department of chemical pathology at St Mary's Hospital in Paddington was not a man easily troubled, or indeed impressed, except perhaps by a carnation of a particularly vibrant colour or an elegant antique pocket watch. Visitors to his laboratory on the fourth floor of the recently constructed red brick building found him distant and reclusive. As a lecturer in biochemistry, he was not a man to whom students easily warmed. An illustration of his solitary nature was that, despite being a keen and distinguished Freemason, he refused to join the hospital's own lodge, preferring instead to maintain a strict separation between his work and personal life. At home in Bath Street, Slough, Dr Lynch shared his life with his wife and young daughter and indulged his passion for fine wine and 'crime, clocks and carnations', blooms of the latter persistently protruding from his buttonhole. At work, however, he was as silent as the grave with whose contents he so often had to deal.

The good doctor was involved in crime as he was the latest in a distinguished line of medical men who established, by dint of their expertise and careful clinical procedures, the place of pathology and medical jurisprudence in English law. The pioneer of forensic detection was Sir William Wilcox, who first earned the title 'the king's poisoner' on account of his expert testimony in identifying the fatal substance used by the mass murderer Dr Hawley Harvey Crippen in 1923. The official title was Senior Official Analyst for the Home Office, but the moniker was handed down, like a trusty bottle of arsenic, to each of his successors including, by 1941, Dr Roche Lynch.

Scotland Yard first contacted Dr Lynch with concerns over the Prime Minister's cigars in March. Winston Churchill had been presented with a gift of two large boxes of cigars sent by a Cuban workers organization known as the 'Antonio Camaguey Society'. The boxes were labelled: 'A present to Mister Churchill from the Society of Antonio Mecco of Camaguey, Cuba, as proof of the sympathy of this institution for the great English nation.'

Upon receipt of the cigars, J. Balfour of the Foreign Office had forwarded them to Sir Norman Kendal at Scotland Yard with a note: 'While we have no reason to doubt the good faith of the donors of these cigars, it occurs to us that this particular form of present offers considerable scope to any enemy of the prime minister who might wish to try his hand at poisoning . . .'

In a time of war failure to act can prove fatal, so Mr Balfour's concern was prudent. Cuba, while distant from the theatre of war, was not untouched. German spies had long been suspected of operating on the island and U-boats had been spotted off the coast, prompting the island's most famous resident, Ernest Hemingway, to fit a machine gun on the bow of his fishing boat, the *Pilar*, and conduct regular, if unsuccessful, scouting patrols.

When Dr Roche received the cigars, which he considered unsightly enough to describe as 'fearsome articles', he took the liberty of calling an old friend from St Paul's School who was now a senior partner in one of 'the largest importers of cigars in the country'. After a careful examination and a brief smoke, the friend concluded that they comprised 'a quite good quality tobacco' considering that its origins lay in an area not known for the quality of its yield. On grounds of taste the cigars were adequate, but what of their safety? Dr Roche's friend had certainly not fallen to the floor, but this meant nothing. He stated: 'It is impossible for me to test the cigars for every known poison, especially when it is possible that they could have been treated with some tropical poison not seen in this country.' He did, however, perform a number of routine tests, without revealing the hand of any assassin. Yet still he was unhappy: 'If any attempt on the life of anyone is to be made with cigars, I would suggest that the poison is not likely to be inhaled in the smoke as the heat of combustion would destroy nearly all the poison. I do, however, suggest that such a happening is possible from incorporating the poison in the mouth end of the cigar. Quite a number of poisons have a fatal dose of less than one grain and such a poison could be administered in such a way.'

Like all his fellow countrymen, Lynch was aware of Churchill's incessant chomping: 'From photographs of the P.M. I should say he probably chews the end of the cigar which would make this possibility more easy.' As a scientist Lynch felt his work was inconclusive and so he added a note of polite concern: '[The P.M.] should be advised not to smoke any cigars which are sent to him unless the source is absolutely beyond doubt.'

The report sent to Sir Norman Kendal was what the Scotland Yard officer had wanted to hear. The message which he in turn passed on to the Foreign Office conceded that: 'Whilst we must agree that the risk of poison is infinitesimal, I do not think that the Prime Minister ought to take it.'

Concealing the arrival of two boxes of indifferent cigars for Winston Churchill – who, having completed the final negotiations with America for the Lend-Lease programmes, was now ordering directives to break German superiority in the Atlantic – was achieved with relative ease. The next consignment from Cuba was a good deal more desirable and concealing it, or persuading the Prime Minister to exercise restraint, was to prove impossible.

On 27 March 1941, the British Ambassador to Cuba, Sir G. Ogilvie Forbes, was informed by the Cuban Minister for Foreign Affairs that the Cuban National Commission of Tobacco, of which the minister was a member, had prepared a gift for the Prime Minister 'in recognition of his services to the causes of democracy'. It was a beautiful mahogany cabinet, 5 feet tall, containing 2,400 of the island's finest cigars, which they estimated was one year's supply. A similar cabinet was dispatched to President Roosevelt, who unfortunately smoked only cigarettes. Forbes made clear in a telegram that, in his opinion, the gift was 'impossible to refuse' and that the donors were opposed to the cigars being passed directly on to the Red Cross, as unwanted gifts often were. In fact, to nudge the British Government's hand towards acceptance and to block this avenue, the Tobacco Commission had already dispatched a sizeable donation of cigarettes to the Red Cross. The Government reluctantly agreed and on 8 April 1941, at the official presentation in the offices of the Cuban National Commission of Tobacco in Havana, Sir Ogilvie Forbes saw what a truly striking gift had been given. The cabinet had exquisite marquetry and its doors opened to reveal six shelves, on each of which sat four wooden boxes marked with the exclusive brands they contained: H. Upmann, Por Larranaga, Ramon Allones, Romeo y Julieta, El Rey del Mundo and Hoyo de Monterrey. The next day Sir Ogilvie Forbes cabled to Anthony Eden, the Foreign Secretary: 'The whole proceedings were very cordial and regret at the suspension of the tobacco trade with Great Britain was quite overcome by the expressions of admiration for Mr Churchill and for Britain's part in the war.'

Winston Churchill was informed of the gift in a memo on 22 April from John (Jock) Colville, who sought the Prime Minister's permission to respond with a note of thanks, though he warned that Scotland Yard had advised against smoking cigars given as gifts: 'They say that any noxious substance could have been added to the cigars during the process of manufacture, and it would only be practicable to examine chemically a limited number of them.'

No one in the British Government, with the obvious exception of Winston Churchill himself, wanted the Prime Minister to smoke the cigars on their arrival. As the cabinet was now in the hold of a Red Cross ship travelling to Britain via America, Winston's concerned colleagues had a little time to examine their options and wasted none of it. On the evening of 21 April 1941, Jock Colville met with Brendan Bracken to discuss what to do. Bracken was blunt. In his opinion the very existence of the cigars should be hidden; if Churchill did not know about them, he surely could not smoke. Colville, however, disagreed and later wrote a memo to Eric Seal, the principal private secretary: 'When these arrive, I think it will be very difficult to do as Mr Bracken suggested and suppress them! The Prime Minister is quite likely to ask what has become of them and in any case they represent a gift of considerable value. Would it not be best for you to ask Mr Bracken and Mrs Churchill to represent to the Prime Minister that they should not be smoked?' The following day Eric Seal sent a handwritten note to Professor Lindemann, Churchill's close friend and scientific adviser, which concluded: 'In short, is there any watertight examination by means of which we could make sure the cigars are OK?'

The man on whose shoulders fell the weight of responsibility for securing the safety of Churchill's cigars was Victor Rothschild. He was a keen cricketer, who as head of the counter-sabotage section of MI5 discovered that his tasks included batting off any balls bowled by Germany at the stumps made by the Prime

Minister's cigars. It was an unusual role for a scientist whose area of expertise was the sex life of frogs, but the precision he brought from the dissection table would serve him well.* Yet in 1941 he was still tracing the boundaries of his new role and disappointed to discover that it rendered him a medieval taster to Britain's political 'King'. The only son of Charles Rothschild, the banker and naturalist, he was at school at Harrow when his father committed suicide in 1923. At Cambridge University he drove fast cars, was an accomplished jazz pianist and began to amass what would become the largest collection of eighteenth-century books in private hands. He also, to his subsequent regret, joined the Apostles alongside the notorious Soviet spies Anthony Blunt and Guy Burgess, a decision that darkened his twilight years after both men were unmasked and a false rumour spread that he was the 'Third Man'.

After discussions with Professor Lindemann, Lord Rothschild – albeit somewhat reluctantly – took on the task of ensuring the security of Churchill's cigars. The issue of the Prime Minister's safety as regards the cigars had preyed on his mind, but he had remained silent 'partly from fear of being considered melodramatic' and

---

* In 1944 his calm defusing of a new type of German bomb found in a cargo of British onions won him the George Medal.

also out of a breakdown in communication over whose responsibility the cigars came under. Prior to May 1941, Scotland Yard had been responsible for ensuring their safety and for intercepting other gifts such as chocolates that were also susceptible to poisoning.

There then followed a comical exchange of letters between Jock Colville and Rothschild over Churchill's chocolates. On 2 June 1941, Colville wrote:

> Do you think it would be desirable that we should in future send you small boxes of cigars, chocolates and other things of the same kind instead of sending them to Scotland Yard? In the past such things have been given to the Prime Minister's detective, Inspector Thompson, and have, as far as I can make out, never emerged again from the Yard. If we send them to you, I feel more certain that they were properly examined, and we might also stand a better chance of getting them back if they were innocuous!'

Rothschild replied two days later to request the cigars but hold the chocolates: 'I do not see very much point in your sending chocolates and things of that sort to me instead of to Scotland Yard through Inspector Thompson. I imagine that they eat the chocolates or feed them to dogs and observe the results. In any case I think they would be very hurt at the thought that somebody else was going to do that work.' He explained that MI5 had a 'bacteriological expert on the spot' and that 'I do not think the Yard are qualified for this sort of thing.' He was unaware that MI5's biological expert was one Dr Roche Lynch.

Winston Churchill was eventually informed of the imminent arrival of the Cuban cigars in a note from Jock Colville on 18 June 1941. This was good news after a day of bad. The previous day the Prime Minister had been informed by Sir Archibald Wavell, Commander-in-Chief, Middle East, that the British Army's first major counter-attack in the Western Desert, Operation Battleaxe, had ended in defeat with the destruction of 91 British tanks. Yet even Colville's welcome note was tinged with caution:

I have discussed with the Professor, and also with Lord Rothschild of MI5, the question of security and they both insist that however reputable the source from which the cigars come it is impossible to ensure that they are safe. It would be perfectly possible to insert a grain of deadly poison in, say, one cigar in fifty, and although Lord Rothschild can and will arrange for those that arrive to be X-rayed, he would only guarantee them after subjecting each one to careful analysis. This could not be done without destroying the cigars.

Professor Lindemann was gracious enough to extend the promise that while there might be no jam today there would be lashings tomorrow, as Colville explained: 'The professor thought however that you might like to let them accumulate in a safe and dry place until after the war, when you might feel justified in taking the risk involved in smoking them.'

Churchill believed that no pleasure should be delayed. On 22 June, just hours after learning of Operation Barbarossa, the German invasion of Russia, he dictated a terse memo: 'Let me see them.'

If he wished to see them, he would wish to smoke them.

Meanwhile the cabinet of cigars had arrived in Britain by 20 August and now sat in the Red Cross's bonded warehouse at Hobart House in London. However, before it could be moved there was the small matter of Customs duty. Cigar importation into Britain was prohibited as an unnecessary waste of dollars on a luxury item, and even gifts of cigars were subject to a crippling rate of tax. The duty on 1 lb of cigars was £1. 8 shillings, while the total duty on the entire cabinet was over £50 – six times the average monthly wage at that time. The Treasury had no powers to waive the duty for any citizen, even the Prime Minister, and so their price would have to be paid. The question was, by whom? The most suitable candidate was the Cuban Legation, who were disgruntled to discover the cost of their gift escalating even higher. Worse still, they were also to be denied any publicity from the Prime Minister. The Cuban Ambassador's request for an official presentation at 10 Downing Street was politely refused. A presentation had already taken place in Havana attended by the British Ambassador; besides, the key to the cabinet was now missing. Instead Cuba received only a brief thank-you note and a signed photograph.

On 23 September Churchill was informed that a cigar from each box had been sent to Lord Rothschild for laboratory testing. In fact, while Colville had planned to select the cigars himself, Rothschild insisted on dispatching his own MI5 officer to make the choice. On that date Colville once again warned the Prime Minister against sneaking a sly smoke. 'It is hoped,' he wrote, 'that you will not smoke any of the cigars until the result of the analysis is known . . . there has just been a round-up of undesirable elements in Cuba, which has shown that a surprisingly large number of Nazi agents and sympathizers exist in that country.'

Ten days later, on 3 October, the Prime Minister asked his secretary K. Hill to check if the analysis was complete. F. D. Brown reported that 'a proportion of the cigars have been tested and found free from noxious content' and that a report would be submitted by Lord Rothschild shortly.

On 24 September Dr Lynch had finally taken possession of a total of 47 cigars and quickly set about their dissection. Problems immediately became apparent; it was not enough, he concluded, to test a few samples, but all must be scrutinized in such a manner as would reveal any poisons present while compensating for the one deadly poison he already knew about: nicotine.

There were two areas of study: the end that would eventually be wedged into the Prime Minister's mouth (or 'surface of contact' as it was called) and the trunk of the cigar or 'main substance'. The end that entered the mouth was examined for both bacteriological and chemical abnormalities, while the trunk was scrutinized for 'potentially volatile chemical agents'.

As a control group with which to compare the Cuban samples, Dr Lynch had already purchased a supply of similar-sized Cuban cigars from the tobacconists of London, who would have been distraught to know that instead of being slowly set alight and then savoured, the purchaser planned a more diabolical fate. The cigars were stretched out on a piece of sterile greaseproof paper and then examined by Dr Lynch using a powerful hand-held magnifying glass. Afterwards they were cut with a razor to a length of 1½ inches, re-examined, then sliced open for a final examination. A fraction of the cigar was then cut off and sealed in a sterile test-tube in case any further reference was required.

A sliver from every cigar, both Cuban samples and the control group, was then individually mixed into its own 'nutrient broth', after which approximately 0.6 cc were injected into a selection of mice. No mouse had previously been known for its ability to savour a fine Cuban cigar, but each one succumbed to the sensation familiar to cigar connoisseurs, the delicious narcotic quality of nicotine. Careful testing had revealed that the correct amount of 'broth' would stupefy a mouse into a period of muscular weakness in which it would lie prone – stoned, almost. The effect of a safe cigar, where exposure was restricted to a healthy dose, would last less than an hour after which the creature would recover and eat. Dr Lynch had calibrated the test so that an early death could be read as the result of 'pathogenic bacteria'; in other words, evidence of the assassin's hand.

A second test involved the mice breathing in the smoke from the suspect cigars. Here a single gram of the cigar was burned steadily for a 25–30-minute period and the smoke was then drawn through a glass tube in which sat a mouse, who stoically endured a small degree of carbon dioxide poisoning for the good of his master's Prime Minister.

The testing elicited a number of results, that of most concern being a pair of dead mice. Each animal was monitored for days after the experiments and two succumbed, the first after three days and the other after six. An autopsy was immediately conducted, but the cause of death was traced to a form of food poisoning which had been present in the mouse stock at the time. 'It was clear that the death of these animals was to be attributed to an intercurrent infection and not to the infective or toxic property of the test material,' read Dr Lynch's report.

It was also discovered that three cigars contained foreign bodies of a natural, though far from pleasant, substance: 'One contained a small black and flattened mass of vegetable debris containing much starch and two hairs with the features of those of a mouse: this was almost certainly a faecal pellet from a mouse. One contained a tiny concretion of what appeared to be uncooked maize starch. The third showed a group of tiny oval pellets of vegetable debris; this was obviously the droppings of an insect.'

To conclude his experiments, Dr Lynch placed ever larger slices of the cigar under his own tongue. His conclusion, in a written report delivered to Lord Rothschild, stated: 'I am satisfied that the exhibits examined are toxicologically and bacteriologically normal.'

Winston Churchill could have given the doctor this news six weeks ago.

Under no circumstances could Churchill be described as a cautious man. As a child he leapt off a stone bridge into a nearby tree, missed the branch, fell 20 feet and broke his leg. As a cavalry officer at Omdurman he let off a volley of shots that led to him being chased, hopelessly outnumbered by violent tribesmen. As a politician the old maxim 'look before you leap' clearly did not chime with his own motto: 'Action This Day'.

In truth, Winston Churchill had disregarded both memos and reports and before Lord Rothschild had even received a single cigar, he decided to test the safety of the cigars himself. However, should they have been poisoned, his actions would have cost the country not only himself but the entire Defence Committee. Yet the ultimate beneficiary of his foolhardiness was the Soviet Union.

On the evening of 19 September the Members of the Defence Committee were in a deadlocked debate about what military assistance should be provided to the Russians. While the service ministers and chiefs of staff had insisted that they could not spare even a rowing boat or rifle without weakening Britain's own efforts, Churchill made it clear that a straight refusal was not an option. Each service would have to shave something from their supplies, but the debate dragged on over exactly what this should be. The Prime Minister vowed to keep everyone at the table all night – though pausing, of course, for a two-hour dinner with Clemmie. Instead of returning to the Cabinet Room, he ushered the committee into a small anteroom to the left of Downing Street's hall and proudly displayed his new cigar collection.

'See, this came for me today. I have had some difficulty getting this through Customs,' he said, then began pulling out bundles of long Romeo y Julieta, H. Upmann and Por Larranaga.

As Lord Balfour, then Under-Secretary of State at the Air Ministry, recalled:

Turning to the waiting Ministers, he addressed us thus, 'Gentlemen, I am now going to try an experiment. Maybe it will result in joy. Maybe it will end in grief. I am about to give you each one of these magnificent cigars.' He paused, then continued with Churchillian effect, 'It may well be that these each contain some deadly poison.' He went on, alluding to the possible act of poisoning the entire Defence Committee: 'It may well be that within days I shall follow sadly the long line of coffins up the aisle of Westminster Abbey. Reviled by the populace, as the man who has out Borgia-ed Borgia.'

Each committee member returned to the Cabinet Room contentedly puffing a rare Havana cigar. As the room clouded up, so tempers calmed down and the atmosphere became conducive to progress. Otto von Bismarck, founder of the German empire against which they were now embattled, said of cigars: 'A cigar is a sort of diversion: as the blue smoke curls upwards, the eye involuntarily follows it; the effect is soothing, one feels better tempered, and more inclined to make concessions.' As Harold Balfour recalled: 'In half an hour we had settled all we had argued about for hours. Russian aid was safe and firm.'

Winston's joke about having 'out Borgia-ed Borgia' was proof that he regarded the scrupulous work of Rothschild and his team as unnecessary. He had clearly concluded that the chance of a poison-loaded rogue cigar reaching his mouth was so remote as to be dismissed. While he would play along with his staff's concerns, when the opportunity presented itself he dismissed them out of hand and took action on his own.

In Nazi Germany tobacco products were viewed with contempt. A popular poster campaign at the time featured a smoker's head being crushed under the heel of a jackboot, and on countless occasions Adolf Hitler must have wished that smoker to be Winston Churchill. For the expansive differences between the two men, democrat to dictator, also included the matter of smoking. The supposed teetotal vegetarian, who may have viewed his body as a sacred temple while reducing others to ash, was an obstinate anti-smoker under whose regime the first scientific anti-smoking initiatives were carried out. In 1939 Franz H. Muller was the first scientist to use case-control epidemiological methods to document the relationship between smoking and lung cancer. Hitler was the 'pin-up' illustrating the healthier life. In 1937 he posed on the cover of *Auf der Wacht*, a German magazine that carried the caption: 'Our Fuhrer Adolf Hitler drinks no alcohol and does not smoke . . . His performance at work is incredible.' A natural retort to such German boasts is to be found in Winston Churchill's quip to General Montgomery, who shared a number of Hitler's attitudes to healthy living and who once declared: 'I do not drink, I do not smoke, I sleep a great deal. That is why I am 100 per cent fit.' Churchill responded: 'I drink a great deal, I sleep a little, and I smoke cigar after cigar. That is why I am 200 per cent fit.'

Hitler's aversion to cigarettes and cigars sprang from his childhood when he was punished for smoking an illicit cigarette while at school, and continued when he was too poor to smoke in Vienna during his unsuccessful struggle to become an artist. In Germany under the Reich, smoking was frowned upon though impossible to ban. In speeches Hitler described tobacco as 'the wrath of the Red man against the White man for having given them hard liquor'. Members of the Nazi Women's League pledged not to smoke any tobacco products lest it harm their duty to swell the master race. In a move which foreshadowed California by sixty years, smoking was banned in public places and on transport, while pregnant women were forbidden from smoking as were members of the Luftwaffe – an exception being made for Goering and his cigars. As a result, during the Second World War the regular German soldier received the lowest daily cigarette ration of all the combatants: just six per day. Cigars were usually restricted to the officer classes, and were particularly popular among the SS. British soldiers, surprisingly for a country so addicted to the weed, were allocated just seven, while the Americans were positively profligate, equipping their men with enough packs to provide between fifteen and twenty cigarettes daily. The Russians, meanwhile, preferred to roll their own, using newsprint to enhance the flavour.

For the soldier on the march, a tank commander or combat pilot, the act of smoking was an important part of war. It was a brief recreation, uniting men in a common activity and, most importantly, it calmed – however slightly – nerves taut enough to snap. A GI on the beach at Normandy explained: 'A guy in war has to have some outlet for his nerves and I guess smoking is as good as anything.'

Churchill thought so too.

In late October a second batch of cigars, this time a gift from admirers in Brazil, was tested before being reluctantly passed for consumption. While Lord Rothschild wrote that 'it would be safer to smoke the rest than to cross a London street', he was still troubled by what he saw as a needless risk. In a letter to F.D. Brown he suggested exchanging smaller gifts of cigars for a fresh, safe batch from a London store: 'I suggest the exchange principle because I must say I think it rather irritating to receive a present of this sort and not have any benefit out of it. I would like to recommend the principle that gifts consisting of small numbers should automatically be treated by the substitution method, while special gifts . . . be subjected to the detailed examination.'

The idea was supported, in poetical form, in a note to Winston Churchill written by Sir John Martin, dated 7 November 1941: 'All these suggestions may seem illogical in implying that the risk is so small that the cigars may be smoked by other people but not by yourself; but

I hope you will agree, for the reason that (if you will excuse the parody):

> *A breath could make them, as a breath unmade;*
> *But the Prime Minister, their country's pride,*
> *If once destroyed can never be supplied*

Churchill was not impressed, by either the poetry or the suggestion posed. He replied tersely: 'If these cigars are not thought safe for me, they are not safe for anyone and had better be destroyed.'

Problems continued to arise from presents. For example, when Churchill was sent a Stilton cheese by a Mr J. Arthur Goulburn, a Manchester cheesemonger, he thought it only gracious to thank him by sending a signed copy of his book *Great Contemporaries*. Unfortunately Mr Goulburn spun his offer of the cheese into an 'order' from the Prime Minister which he then advertised in his shop window. An angry competitor wrote to explain that Mr Goulburn was advertising to the effect that he had executed with pleasure an order from Mr Churchill of one whole 'Old Windsor' Stilton cheese.

The dark interior of the Robert Lewis tobacconist shop at the turn of
the century, where Winston Churchill first visited in 1900 and became
a loyal customer, placing his final order on 23 December 1964.

(*JJ Fox & Robert Lewis*)

Customer orders were meticulously recorded: Winston Churchill
began a life-long relationship by ordering 50 Bock Giraldas,
small Havana cigars, for £4. (*JJ Fox & Robert Lewis*)

Churchill relaxing with his daughter, Mary, at Chartwell in 1922, shortly after he had purchased the house in the Kent countryside, where he stored as many as 3,000 cigars.

(The Estate of Winston Churchill)

The pair behind Robert Lewis: Jose de Sola Pinto (*right*), known as the 'Ostrich' for his unhelpful approach to business problems, was balanced by the wise head of Fred Croley (*left*).

(JJ Fox & Robert Lewis)

Joaquin Cuesta insisted on putting his face to the cigars that his small
Havana factory made for Winston Churchill. Antonio Giraudier took
it off, believing it annoyed the Prime Minister.

Cigars were a constant aid to relaxation for Churchill:
here with his brother Jack, son Randolph and nephew John,
enjoying a visit to Calgary in 1927.

(The Estate of Winston Churchill)

Dr Gerald Roche Lynch, protector of the prime minister's cigars, devised stringent procedures (including tests on mice) to ensure that Churchill's supplies were free from any trace of Nazi poison.

(*Society of Apothecaries*)

THE CHURCHILL CIGAR

5 YESTERDAY I asked what had happened to the cigar which Mr. Churchill laid on the edge of the wagon when he addressed the crowd in St. George's Square.

I remarked that it had disappeared under the noses of some determined souvenir hunters. Well, here is the story of its subsequent adventures, as related to me today.

As Mr. Churchill took his leave the cigar fell from the wagon on to the ground, and a seventeen-year-old boy, a plumber's appprentice, who had had his eye on it all the time, dived for it. He collided with a man bent on the same mission, and soon both had hold of the Churchill Havana. Neither would relinquish the prize, but a compromise was effected, the celebrated cigar was cut in two and the youth took one half, and the man the other.

The youth hurried home with his prize, which was relighted. He took one draw at it and then handed it to his father, who also took a draw. The cigar was then put away to be preserved as a historic souvenir.

The public's desire to secure a souvenir of Churchill's cigar almost resulted in fights, as reported by one local paper.

(*Huddersfield Examiner*)

A 101-foot structure made from galvanized steel and aluminium sheeting, erected in the Australian town of Churchill, instantly became known as 'The Big Cigar'. It remains a tourist attraction to this day.
(*Latrobe Valley Express*)

The secret to success is a cigar. When Winston Churchill was voted Greatest Briton, followed by Isambard Kingdom Brunel, Hunters & Frankau ran this cheeky advert.
(*Hunters & Frankau*)

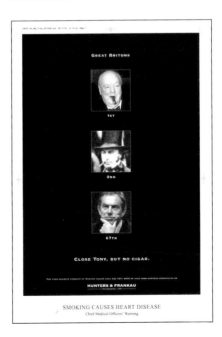

GREAT BRITONS

1ST

2ND

67TH

CLOSE TONY, BUT NO CIGAR.

HUNTERS & FRANKAU

SMOKING CAUSES HEART DISEASE
Chief Medical Officers' Warning

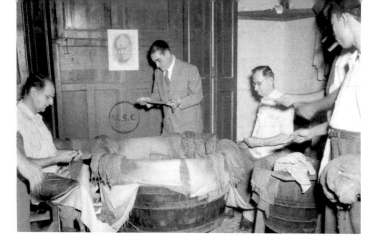

Big Brother is watching:
Antonio Giraudier
arranged for sixteen
photographs to be taken
documenting the prepara-
tion of Winston Churchill's
cigars. Joaquin Cuesta, the
factory owner, believed his
staff would be inspired by
a visual reminder of their
greatest customer.

(*Churchill Archives Centre*)

Cigar gifts were constant, but still delighted Winston Churchill, here being presented with one in 1951. (*Churchill Archives Centre*)

Winston Churchill's painting *Bottlescape*, completed on Boxing Day 1926, balanced champagne bottles and a cigar box in a tribute to the good life. (*Reproduced with permission of Anthea Morton-Saner on behalf of Churchill Heritage Ltd. Copyright © Churchill Heritage Ltd*)

In 1941, a gift from the Cuban Government of an ornate mahogany cabinet containing 2,400 of the finest cigars triggered a major security alert, as MI5 struggled to ensure they were safe enough for the Prime Minister to smoke. (*Churchill Archives Centre*)

The mellow smoke of a fine cigar often surrounded Churchill while he painted.

What made this even more problematical was that Lord Woolton and the Ministry of Food had recently asked people not to eat cheese so as to leave it for the consumption of manual workers.

The question of how to handle Mr Goulburn's deception became academic when the shopkeeper wrote to apologize for the delay in thanking the Prime Minister for his present, as he had been rather busy: 'Unfortunately my food store was completely demolished during the recent aerial bombardment of Manchester; nevertheless we in Manchester remain "grave but gay".'

While government staff urged a blanket ban on the acceptance of all gifts for ease of administration, Winston felt that this would be rude and inconsiderate and instead decreed that each gift should be examined on a case-by-case basis. On 11 January 1941, a memo was prepared specifically on the matter of gifts of cigars. This read: 'As regards cigars, the Prime Minister thinks it would be ungracious to refuse all such presents. In order to safeguard the Prime Minister and check up on the sender we will however arrange for acknowledgements of such gifts from abroad to be sent through the Embassy or Consulate or, in the case of a dominion, through our High Commissioner.'

The security aspect was also raised:

We should endeavour to check up on the bona fides of the donors and if accepted the question of examination of cigars must be raised. In regard to cigars, three points would arise:

1. Where the senders are reputable and the cigars are good, the Prime Minister would accept the cigars (and would pay the duty if from abroad).

2. Where the senders are reputable but the cigars are not fit to smoke, cigars could be sent to hospitals but the Prime Minister should not pay the duty.

3. Where the cigars have only been sent for purposes of advertisement or some similar object they should not be accepted (unless in special cases, they should not be sent back to the owners if abroad; they might be sent to hospitals here).

Food and cigars were crucial to Winston Churchill – they were like coal in a furnace, fuel to power his titanic fight. In the closing months of 1941, just as America was on the verge of being dragged into the fray, a New York businessman took on the job of ensuring that the Prime Minister of Great Britain would not lack for his principal creature comfort and, in the process, created the first 'Churchill cigar'.

FOUR

—

THE CHURCHILL CIGAR

'Those wonderful cigars have cheered
my long path through war.'

Winston Churchill

THE CHRISTMAS TREE on the South Lawn of the White House glowed as warmly as the friendship between the two men who had lit it. The turbulent courtship between Winston Spencer Churchill and Franklin Delano Roosevelt was over. The attack on Pearl Harbor on 7 December 1941 had brought the might of America into the war and Prime Minister and President into a marriage of convenience. The festive period would mark their short, sweet honeymoon before the strains of partnership began to pull them apart. 'No lover ever studied every whim of his mistress as I did those of President Roosevelt,' said Churchill of the politician he described as 'the greatest man I have ever known'. Roosevelt, as the more powerful and restrained partner, said of Churchill, 'He's really absolutely sweet.'

Winston had arrived in Washington on 22 December anxious to persuade the President that Germany under Adolf Hitler was where the true fight must be fought, not in the Pacific, so he was delighted to discover that Roosevelt and his generals shared the view that the Nazis rather than Nippon were the 'long-term threat'. With the principal hurdle quickly cleared, the Prime Minister could relax and enjoy the adulation of the American people, address Congress to acclaim and delight in the extensive menus and specially imported brandies of a most hospitable White House. 'He ate, and thoroughly enjoyed more food than any two men or three diplomats,' recalled a member of staff. 'He consumed brandy and Scotch with a grace and enthusiasm that left us all open-mouthed in awe.'

To the Secret Service who each day took charge of mountainous boxes, it seemed that the entire population of America wished to provide Winston Churchill with his cigars. Walter Thompson, Churchill's bodyguard, had previously commented that the destruction of perfectly safe cigars in Downing Street was 'sad'; upon reaching the White House, he revised his assessment to 'tragic', such was the volume. He recalled:

'Each day, from all over North America and South America and from hundreds of West Indies Islands came uncountable boxes of the finest cigars ever made. Hundreds of thousands of them went right into the White House incinerator. Others often smoked them or took them home. But never Winston. And none of the White House staff was permitted to smoke them anywhere in the District of Columbia. [He added] But I never heard of one exploding.

In fact, Winston did collect a box of cigars which were delivered to the White House during his stay and, in truth, given the unwelcome guests it contained, it might have been better had it exploded. On Christmas Eve, after Churchill and Roosevelt had lit the tree, the Prime Minister returned to his room to find a letter from Carter Glass, a US senator, with a wrapped box of La Corona cigars. Senator Glass was 5 feet 4 inches tall, with a ruined digestive system but a hearty appetite for politics. He was born in 1858 in Virginia, the antebellum south, and Roosevelt – with whom he had worked closely – described him as 'an unreconstructed rebel'. Glass had fought all his political life to keep white landed gentry firmly upon the top of the heap and he

viewed Winston Churchill as a kindred spirit. His letter
read:

'My Dear Mr Churchill,

Some months back, my very dear friend Sam
Kaplan of New York City, through the British
Ambassador, Lord Halifax, managed to get through
to you some extra fine cigars, especially made for
you of the finest Havana, and carrying the imprimatur of your illustrious name. Your acknow-
ledgement of receipt and thanks is now framed and
cherished on his walls at No. 7 Vestry Street, New
York City.

At the time there were more made up than he
could send, and now that you are in this country,
happily for all of us, he wants you to have them,
and I have undertaken the pleasant mission of
seeing that they get in your hands.

In so doing, may I not add a personal note of
warmth and gratitude to you, for the great service
you are rendering the cause of freedom and free
men everywhere, and to say to you that your very
presence on these shores, brief as it may be, makes
the torch of liberty burn brighter in every American
heart.

Samuel Kaplan was a successful Jewish businessman from New York who had heard (via Carter Glass) from Lord Halifax, the new British Ambassador to America, that the Prime Minister's own stock of Havana cigars was dwindling. As there would be no more legal importations planned until the war had been won, Kaplan set about ensuring that until then his hero would not lack for a quality smoke. In late 1940 he immediately dispatched his daughter and son-in-law, Ralph Rubinger, to Havana where they were evidently taken by the colourful adverts that ran in *Who's Who Havana Club* magazine, a society journal popular among the visiting Americans: 'For the best cigars ask for La Corona – and do not be misled.' The advert continued: 'The worldwide fame of these famous cigars results in their being imitated more than other brands. For your protection see that you secure the genuine "La Corona" brand, every box of which carries the seal.'

The couple returned with 5,000 cigars, seal and all.

On 27 December, the day following Churchill's electrifying address to Congress, he dictated a short note of thanks to Samuel Kaplan on White House stationery:

'My Dear Mr Kaplan,
Thank you so much for your Christmas greetings

and for the cigars which Senator Glass has safely handed to me. I can assure you that their forerunners were quite the best that I ever smoked and look forward indeed to this new batch.

[He then added in his own hand] It is so kind of you to think of me and [a] very sweet compliment that the bands bear my name over them. Once more thanks, believe me . . . yours sincerely, Winston Churchill.

There is evidence to suggest that, despite Churchill's charming letter, Kaplan's gift was much the worse for wear when finally opened. After the demands of Washington Winston had enjoyed a brief break in Palm Beach at the home of Edward Stettinius, administrator of the Lend-Lease programme, where he swam in the nude and scared a shark, recalling: 'My bulk must have frightened him away.' He returned to the White House, and on 13 January 1942 joined Roosevelt for a dinner which was attended by (among others) Margaret Hambley. In a letter she described Churchill's conversation as wonderfully colourful. Apparently Churchill said how terrible it was of Hitler to '. . . bomb all the beautiful Scotch whisky and cigar warehouses. He said he didn't know what would happen to a country when its supplies of whisky and cigars ran out.'

Churchill, accompanied by President Roosevelt, then described the arrival of a Christmas present of a box of Cuban cigars which, unfortunately, 'was filled with worms'. Although the suggestion made Hambley feel quite ill, Churchill – enjoying his childish humour – continued to talk on. 'He seemed to delight in my ill-ness and went into more & more detail of how they crept through each cigar.'

It is impossible to say for certain if the cigars Churchill was referring to were those sent by Samuel Kaplan. However, the evidence is supportive; while hun-dreds of boxes were sent to the Prime Minister at the White House, he was only likely to come into contact with those from recognized names. Yet if they were, unfortunately, Mr Kaplan's, the surprise did not put the Prime Minister off them for good. And, unbeknown to Mr Kaplan, they were later put to a more diplomatic use.

The confidence that is conveyed by a cigar was never more crucial than in the midst of war as Sir Martin Gilbert, Churchill's official biographer, made clear. He explained that in early 1943 Churchill visited President Ismet Inonu of Turkey in a bid to persuade him not to side with Germany:

When I visited President Ismet Inonu in Ankara in 1969, he told me that at his meeting with Churchill in early 1943, he, Inonu, had commented on how harsh the wartime austerity was in Britain. Unknown to Inonu, Churchill had been shown by British Intelligence the text of the telegrams sent to Inonu from the Turkish Ambassador in London that told of how difficult wartime conditions were. Churchill, with his most charming smile, said to President Inonu, 'Ah yes, very difficult times indeed' and then, pulling out of his pocket an incredibly long cigar, added: 'We are even down to the *tiniest* cigars.'

Churchill's cigar, or rather the absence of it, was to result in the most celebrated photograph of the Prime Minister, and one of the most reproduced portraits in photographic history. The encounter between Winston and the Armenian photographer Yousuf Karsh, then resident in Canada, took place on 31 December 1941 at the Canadian House of Commons in Ottawa. Churchill, who had left Washington in order to visit Mackenzie King, the Canadian Prime Minister, had agreed to give Karsh exactly two minutes of his time. His mood was not good. Churchill was unaware that he had suffered a mild heart attack four days earlier which Sir Charles Wilson (later Lord Moran), his personal doctor, had kept from him on grounds that it would do no good to add to his worries a condition over which he had no control. As Karsh recalled: '. . . two niggardly minutes in which I must try to put on film a man who had already written or inspired a library of books, baffled all his biographers, filled the world with his fame, and me, on this occasion, with dread.'

Churchill had marched into the room with a scowl etched on his face and, as Karsh recalled, '. . . regarding my camera as he might regard the German enemy.' Dressed in a dark suit and waistcoat, the only contrast coming from his white shirt, pocket handkerchief and the few speckles of white from his bow-tie, Winston was also chewing a cigar. To the eye of an artist such as Karsh, the cigar had to go, but how? A request could be denied while precious seconds ticked past spent in futile argument; instead, bold action was required and so the photographer simply reached over and snatched the cigar from the Prime Minister's mouth as if taking a dummy from a child. An infant would then have bawled; Churchill's 'scowl deepened, the head was thrust forward belligerently and the hand placed on the hip in an attitude of anger'.

Yet Churchill recognized Karsh's game, and so the next frames recorded a warm smile. As Winston then said, 'You can even make a roaring lion stand still to be photographed,' and so gave the portrait its title: 'The Roaring Lion'.

Finished prints were sent to the White House nine days later, along with a note from Mackenzie King which read: 'I think you will agree that the photograph is one of the best, if not the very best, ever taken of yourself. I, at least, am so inclined to view it.' He enclosed Karsh's address in case Churchill wished to thank him for his achievement, but he did not. In fact in his reply to King, Churchill made no mention of the photographs, but he did thank the Prime Minister for the gift of a white polar-bear skin.

The custodian of Churchill's cigars on all foreign trips was Frank Sawyer. The Prime Minister's valet was a small, balding man from Cumbria, with a round florid face, a pronounced lisp and, as a confirmed bachelor, a mildly camp manner. He was also devoted to Churchill, and his diligence and long hours were matched only by his ability to withstand the full bluster of Churchill's rages as if they were but a summer breeze. In a number of ways he fulfilled the role of Winston's nanny, Mrs Everest; he encouraged him to take a bath and if he spotted that the Prime Minister was on the verge of exhaustion, he ushered him off to bed (which Churchill would usually heed with good grace). Sawyer was popular with the other staff, sneaking the secretaries a glass of champagne where possible. He would work around the clock, pressing suits, sourcing needs, anything to ease the strain on his master, although he was not above playing the occasional prank, or maybe honest mistake, such as the time when, on an Atlantic crossing, he put liquid shoe polish on Churchill's toothbrush with which Winston then cleaned his teeth. Sawyer accompanied Churchill on every foreign visit during the war years; he got lost in a Cairo bazaar and was toasted in the Kremlin by Stalin. Among the archives is a copy of his expenses. During one visit to America he purchased 25 cigars at a cost of $12, the 25 long-stemmed matches coming to a further 25 cents. Sawyer was also in charge of the cigars stored at Chequers, the Prime Minister's rural retreat. A summary of the accounts reads:

Cigars: It is difficult to assess the increase in cost owing to official entertaining at Chequers, as Mr Churchill has for some time past been drawing upon his own private stock including presentation cigars. I estimate that an average of 10 pounds worth of cigars are consumed during each weekend by official guests.

After the war Frank Sawyer would retire from Winston Churchill's service and vanish, like smoke in the wind.

A third batch of Samuel Kaplan's cigars arrived at the British Embassy on 28 May 1943, three days after Churchill and Roosevelt had completed talks in Washington on the location and date of the following year's D-Day landings. These cigars, 150 La Coronas which once again bore the Prime Minister's name, were sent on to London by sea bag. An indication of the esteem in which Churchill now held Kaplan's cigars was that this time he insisted on sending a signed copy of *The World Crisis*, his multi-volume history of the First World War. The accompanying note read: 'I am very much looking forward to receiving the cigars, I know I shall enjoy smoking them.'

Yet another batch was delivered, this time in celebration of the surrender of Italy. In a letter Senator Carter Glass wrote: 'Our mutual good friend, Sam Kaplan . . . thinks that you should have some Winston

Churchill cigars to celebrate the first unconditional surrender and the downfall of the first Hitler puppet . . . I hope you will enjoy every one of them and from each one you will gather renewed strength to help you bear the heavy load ahead.'

More arrived the following January, which prompted Churchill to dispatch three leather-bound volumes of his speeches. This then triggered Kaplan, in a fit of escalation, to send yet more cigars, as Halifax reported: '. . . bigger and better than ever.' Of Churchill's speeches, Kaplan trilled: 'Like the speeches of our own Abraham Lincoln they possess not only eloquence but a simplicity that brings them within the comprehension of every intelligence from the lowliest to the highest.'

The arrival of the bound speeches had also emboldened Kaplan to request a signed photograph which, upon eventual arrival, produced an even greater outpouring of praise:

I am particularly touched that at this most momentous and crucial period in the world's history, in which you so dominantly figure, you were gracious enough to take even a few minutes of your precious time, to comply with my request. May I say that this is one of the aspects of your many-faceted character – the attention of little courtesies amidst world-shaking matters – that has made you one of history's most distinguished personalities.

Churchill responded to compliments like a cat to firm strokes and a warm fire, yet he did prefer his presents. Kaplan, recognizing this, increased his regular supplies from eight boxes to ten.

The pleasure and quiet pride which Winston Churchill took in his eponymous cigars is to be found in a letter sent to the American businessman on 1 January 1945. Despite news reaching Downing Street that German troops had launched an overnight offensive on Allied positions stretched between Saarbrucken and Strasburg, Churchill was certain that the war in Europe would end this year. His concern was when and at what cost. The cigars puffed on days fraught with fear had been a calming aid; he described them as 'those wonderful cigars with which you have cheered my long path through the war'.

He also revealed that the cigar bands had attracted their own share of admirers: 'You will be interested to know that the bands on which you had my name printed are regarded as souvenirs and gladly accepted wherever I go. The Russian Commissar of the Crimea, once it had been translated to him, snapped up one of these like a hawk and put it in his pocket book,' Churchill explained, before adding, 'This is private.'

In the past Churchill had written to Kaplan by a circuitous route that took in both the British Embassy in Washington and the office of Carter Glass. He now wrote direct to his home, where he sent yet another bound copy of his speeches: *Onward to Victory*. Kaplan was delighted and replied: 'Your most gracious letter has more than recompenses [*sic*] for my slight efforts in sending you the cigars. If they have as you say cheered your long path through war then I am doubly rewarded.'

In the spring of 1945, as victory in Europe marched ever closer, Samuel Kaplan's generosity grew. Cigars, it seemed, were no longer enough for Europe's liberator. On 27 March he contacted the Distillers Agency in Edinburgh, which he had been told by his own New York supplier stocked the finest malt whisky. A dozen bottles of Talisker were dispatched to Downing Street. Content that Winston Churchill had the finest malt to pour down his throat, Kaplan now concerned himself with what the Prime Minister wrapped around his neck. The previous November he instructed his secretary, Anne Rivlin, to write to Churchill's secretary, Miss Hill, to enquire about Churchill's neck-ties. Kaplan had spotted in a newsreel one of the rare instances when Winston wore a knotted tie, as opposed to his familiar bow tie. Concerned lest he lack such a crucial item of his wardrobe, Kaplan had his secretary extend an offer: 'We are fortunate in having some silks from which Mr Kaplan should like to make several bow ties for Mr Churchill. If you should send an old one to me he could have it copied and then send it to you.'

Miss Hill replied that the Prime Minister had not changed his habit of tie, but merely wore the traditional tie while in uniform. Miss Rivlin was persistent, replying that Mr Kaplan wished to ascertain the Prime Minister's collar size. 'If there is any particular pattern or colour to which Mr Churchill is partial I should appreciate this information.'

Kaplan's persistence left Miss Hill in an awkward position, as she later explained to Churchill: 'Mr Kaplan now wishes to send you some bow ties and his secretary has asked me to send out one of your old ties as a sample, or else let her know your collar size and your preference as to colour and design. I do not know, as these are rationed goods, whether you would wish to accept this present.'

Churchill evidently wished to decline and a letter

was sent back by Miss Hill in which the Prime Minister '. . . asks to be excused from accepting this gift.' Yet such was the fear of offending such a trusted supplier that Lord Halifax was asked to contact Senator Glass to smooth Kaplan's feathers should the refusal ruffle them. The British Embassy, however, was swift to stamp on such nonsense, stating: 'We do not think that Mr Kaplan's feelings could possibly be hurt by Churchill's letter.' Instead they forwarded the Prime Minister's letter directly to Kaplan, explaining that Senator Glass was 'very old and infirm' and should not be 'troubled'.

Concern and evasion were in vain, for Kaplan had already made up the bow ties as he saw fit and, as his secretary explained, would be 'very disappointed' in not being able to send them. However, this was a hypothetical situation, since the bow ties were already en route and the Prime Minister had little choice but to accept them.

Three years after their last bounteous gift, the Cuban Government chose to bestow a second batch of Havana cigars on the assumption (which proved correct) that the last consignment of 2,500 had long since gone up in smoke. On 28 March 1945, Churchill was informed that Cuba had 3,000 cigars to present to him and that an appointment had been cleared for their ambassador to make the presentation the following day, shortly after the Prime Minister returned from lunch with the King. At the ceremony it was discovered that 700 cigars were missing, which greatly vexed Churchill. His private secretary had promised him 3,000; the Cuban Ambassador had been informed that 2,500 had been shipped, but only 1,700 were to hand.

The Prime Minister did not take kindly to the 'liberation' of his private supply, and so instructed G.E. Blanck, the Cuban Ambassador, to write to his private secretary with details of the chain of delivery so that an investigation could be launched and the culprits caught. Churchill also insisted that he be personally informed of the outcome.

The facts emerged as follows: two large cases had been dispatched from Cuba, one containing 5,000 cigars for the Red Cross, while the second case of 2,500 cigars was for Churchill. Upon arrival at the Cuban Embassy in Wilton Crescent, the Red Cross case had 'three or four' empty boxes, missing roughly 100 cigars, while 'a considerable empty space' was found in Churchill's case. As Mr Blanck explained to Mr Peck, Churchill's private secretary: 'I am very sorry that I mentioned the fact of their loss to the Prime Minister. I would not have done so but for the fact that I think he had already been told that he would receive the 2,500 cigars.'

Churchill's anxiety that the matter of the missing cigars be cleared up promptly was not limited to the desire for the return of 700 cigars which he might not smoke for months. He knew their retrieval was unlikely, but his concern was to cross out the possibility that the light fingers were British. As Mr Peck explained in a letter to A.R. Ashford, head of the Board of Customs and Excise: 'The Prime Minister has asked that stringent enquiry should be made to ascertain if possible how this loss occurred.' He continued: 'A loss of this kind is in itself serious, but it seems to Mr Churchill particularly desirable to establish if possible the fact that the loss did not occur while the package was in this country, or alternatively if it did occur here, that the cause be traced.'

Two weeks after the presentation Churchill, feeling the wheels of justice were grinding too slowly, called on Inspector Thompson to quicken the pace. 'The Prime Minister wants to know if anything has been found out about the rest of cigars,' read a memo dated 14 April 1945. Three days later Customs and Excise replied with a detailed explanation that appeared to point the finger of suspicion away from Blighty towards Cuba. It appeared that the cigars had landed at Liverpool dock on 21 September 1944. They were examined on arrival, and once again, before delivery to the Cuban Embassy on 29 December 1944, the external boxes had not been tampered with. An investigation into the Red Cross consignment found that the theft had taken place 'before docking and indeed before importation. The joints of the package were observed to be loose when it was landed and [in] an internal examination by our officers the shortage was discovered and allowed for. The attention of the Master of the ship was drawn to the position. He maintained that the case was in exactly the same state as when it was put on board in Cuba.'

The question was, what to do? Rowan sought the advice of Detective Thompson: 'It looks as though the loss must have occurred after 29 December when they were passed from the charge of the Customs to that of the Cubans here. Have you had any previous experience of a case of this kind which might help us in regard to future action? It appears that the only possibility would be to put the police on to an investigation but if this is so it would presumably be necessary to investigate what happened not only while the cigars were between

Liverpool and the Cuban legation, but after they had arrived here.' The note ended: 'This course in either case does seem to present certain difficulties.'

Inspector Thompson's view was that: 'The only possible action is to send the gist of Ashford's reply to the Cuban minister and ask him whether he wishes to instruct the Police . . .' Thompson advised against any unilateral action to find the culprit, Cuban or not, and suggested passing the case to the Foreign Office.

A final report was sent to Churchill on 7 May 1945:

As regards your cigars, the Customs examined the package on arrival and when it was handed to the Cubans, and at neither time was there any evidence of damage or interference, nor is there any evidence of interference while they were in the charge of the Transport Company who were engaged to bring them from Liverpool to London by the Cubans. The package however remained at the Cuban Embassy from early January until it was given to you at the end of March.

If you wish the enquiries to proceed further, it will be necessary to bring in the Police, and if their investigation is to be worthwhile it will be necessary for them to investigate everything, including what happened while the cigars were at the Cuban Embassy.

For the sake of relations with Cuba, the matter of the missing cigars was quietly dropped.

It would be erroneous to give the impression, as may be apparent, that only Cuba and the Americans were concerned about Winston Churchill's cigar supplies. The British public inundated the Prime Minister with cigars and assorted paraphernalia. The following are just a selection of the gifts and letters he received from hundreds of admirers.

Master A. Matthew, a 14-year-old boy, bought three cigars with his pocket money to 'show you the gratitude of just one of the millions of boys in England'. Miss Lucy North, 15, of Wootton Rivers near Marlborough, wrote: 'I have enclosed cigars that I won at a dance last night, held in our own little village, and as they are not any use to me, I thought you would like them as a token. You always seem very much to enjoy your cigars, hoping you will these.' Her letter concludes with a large neatly drawn 'V'. The Seagull Patrol of the 1st Kirby Boy Scouts also sent two cigars.

Rose Morris, from Bayswater, London, sent her dead husband's ashtray along with a handwritten note which said: 'No cigar is good enough for you – I have treasured this ashtray belonging to my late husband for many years but I do hope you did not feel like this naughty boy when you tried your first cigar.' The gift was politely declined by 10 Downing Street; it was sent back along with a letter that read: 'I do not know whether you were aware of it, but I would mention that the ashtray when received in this office had the head connection broken.' Another old lady sent an egg that had been laid with a V sign. She thought it was good luck. So did Churchill, who accepted it.

An 'ordinary man in the street' sent Winston a cigar piercer after reading about the cigar gifts from Havana, while a Joan Mason sent a lighter to 'help light your cigar to the way to victory'. British soldiers even sent captured German cigars to the Prime Minister. Brigadier G.S. Harvie Watt, an MP at the Ministry of Education and Churchill's parliamentary private secretary, passed them on explaining: 'I am no judge of these things, my single experiment with a cigar in my earliest youth having been most disastrous.' The men who captured them had written: 'We do not profess to be cigar smokers or connoisseurs of tobacco leaf, perhaps you would be kind enough to pass them on to Mr Winston Churchill who appears to enjoy cigars.'

Then there was the rather odd case of the baby dressed as Churchill. In February 1945 Mr and Mrs Reyes of Ballymena, County Antrim, dressed their two-year-old child in a miniature three piece suit and bow tie, with walking stick, and finished off the mannequin by wedging a cigar where, by all rights, a dummy should have been. After photographing the child they wrote to the Prime Minister: 'I am enclosing herewith a photograph of my baby, James Francis Reyes, born in London the 14th day of October, 1943 . . . People kept saying how much he resembled you in miniature. After a little talk with my wife, we decided to dress him up to try and see if we could imitate a little Mr Churchill and so get him photographed and we have done it as we thought. Hoping you will accept it, and let us know if you have received it.' Churchill's secretary responded by replying with a brief note of thanks. The tributes to Winston's passion were not always actual cigars. One of the most popular was Billy Cotton and his band's recording, on 8 September 1941, of: 'The Man With The Big Cigar', which includes the fine lyrics: 'One sniff of the Old Havana/we'd follow him right to Fuji-yama.'

Señor Rafael Munoz, editor of a Mexican pro-British paper, organized subscriptions to pay for a presentation of Mexican cigars. Since there was no direct crossing to

Europe these were wrapped in sacking and addressed to the British Consulate-General in New York for passage onwards to London via Liverpool. However, an extra message had been attached en route. On the outside of the case was an extremely grubby envelope addressed in pencil 'For His Excellency'; inside was a rough sheet of paper containing a message that had been attached by the Mexican railway workers: 'To the People of England, Hold faith in God and we shall conquer. At this moment, thirty-five minutes past ten, there are arriving at this frontier post of Nuevo Laredo Tamaulipas Mexico the bodies of Mexican seamen treacherously murdered by the assassins of the Axis. The Mexican people righteously indignant demand justice and we with you will fight until victory or death.' The note was signed: 'Raul Parra Rangel & Enrique S. Ortiz, Employees of the Customs Agency of the National Railways of Mexico.'

The General Cigar Company at 119 West 40th Street in New York – manufacturers of the White Owl cigar, among the best advertised in America, and sponsors of Raymond Gram Swing's famous domestic broadcast – prepared a humidor that carried the Churchill crest engraved in sterling silver. A generous offer, but unfortunately it was declined. The present was prompted by

the fact that Churchill had seemingly smoked their
brand while in Italy. *The Stars and Stripes* dated 25
August 1944 had reported that Churchill smoked the
White Owl brand when he ran out of his own during a
visit to the front.

Among the most charming (and wily) letters to
arrive from cigar aficionados to Winston Churchill was
on 10 March 1943 from Theo Mellum, grower of Registered Seed including 'N.W.D corn, Crookston strain,
Minnesota 13 corn, Haney Strain, Golden Bantam Corn,
Hybrid Corn, Irish Cobler Potatoes, Barley, Mindum
Durum, wheat, anthony oats.' The letter read:

Mr Dear Prime Minister Winston Churchill,
Having listened to you several times over the radio
from various places around the globe, seen your
picture in the newspapers with the tempting cigar
you are smoking and a cheerful pleasant smile on
your face while you are smoking your cigar, of
course is natural to anyone that smokes good cigars.
I for one, smoke only once a day and that is from
morning until evening.

I have told Mrs Mellum time and again, I just
wished that I could exchange a cigar with Prime
Minister Winston Churchill. I am sure they are

good, although I don't suppose we would have any cigars here in United States to compare with the type of cigars that you are smoking. I would love to have a chance to smoke one of your cigars. If I send you a cigar [he then, obviously noting his stinginess amends the letter with ink to read 'a box of'] would you in any form or manner be scared to smoke it, fearing that it might be doped with drugs or poisons? Of course, after they leave my hands I could not guarantee from such danger.

When this victory is won and you are in United States would we be asking too much of you if we asked you to come to Fargo, North Dakota in the Red River Valley in the heart of the bread and butter basket of the world? It would be one of our greatest joys if we in the agricultural area, who are today putting up a gallant fight to produce food to help win the victory. You would be a most hearty welcome person here. We would have a chance to see you and hear your address in person. Should such hopes materialise you can rest assured that we will do everything to make your trip a pleasant one.

I have read considerable about your families activities, particularly one of your daughters activities in London. I salute such a gallant family as you have and which you are proud of without a question.

I realise you are a very, very busy man but whenever you find time to answer this letter it shall be one of the most welcome letters in all my life.

I would like to have an opportunity to send you a box of cigars, if you will let me know what type you use, the light or the dark, mild or strong.

With kindest regards, I am

Yours sincerely, Theo Mellum.

Churchill was rarely restricted from smoking. The RAF were even said to have devised an oxygen mask with a hole through which a cigar could fit, but this does not ring true as the combination of oxygen, a lit cigar and a plane would be more than a little hazardous. However, the RAF were as accommodating as possible. The pilot who flew him to Moscow said: 'He filled the plane with so much smoke we had to open the bomb doors.' There was one occasion, however, when Churchill attended a luncheon for King Ibn Sa'ud of Saudi Arabia in whose royal presence both drinking and smoking were prohibited. Churchill's argument was that one man's religious prohibition was another's religious necessity, as he then explained: 'As I was the host, I raised the matter at once, and said to the interpreter that if it was the religion of His Majesty to deprive himself of smoking and alcohol I must point out that my rule of life prescribed as an absolutely sacred rite smoking cigars and also the drinking of alcohol before, after and, if need be, during all meals and in the intervals between them. The King graciously accepted the position.'

Six years of total war and the growing reality of Soviet domination of Eastern Europe had left Winston Churchill physically exhausted and deeply depressed, even as the morning of Victory in Europe – VE Day – dawned. In previous weeks his morale had sunk and his general health, even for a man of seventy, was poor. He had taken to 'working in bed', a scenario in which 'bed' was more important than 'work', and his appetite for paperwork, through which he once happily chomped, had waned considerably. Jock Colville, his private secretary, noted in his diary on 23 April 1945: 'The PM's box is a ghastly state. He does little work and talks too long.'

Yet on that golden morning of 8 May he roused his

old spirit for a long day of public affection. He lunched enthusiastically with the King and then, on the stroke of 3 p.m., he delivered his victory broadcast, a statement he subsequently repeated in the House of Commons. There followed a service of thanksgiving at St Margarets, after which he returned to the Commons smoking room. Later in the car, on the short drive to Buckingham Palace, he asked Inspector Thompson for a cigar, but his bodyguard had forgotten his case. As Thompson recorded in his memoirs: 'He was quite charming: "Let us go round to the annexe, I will get one there." I thought he must have wanted to smoke very badly indeed, but should have known better, and did, thanks to his next sentence: "I must put on a cigar. They expect it."'

The Potsdam conference in July would be Churchill's final appearance as a wartime Prime Minister as Britain, Russia and America met for the third time – after Teheran and Yalta – in the Cecilienhof Palace, outside Berlin. On the opening day Stalin was seen to have momentarily ditched his pipe, one of which was a present from Churchill, purchased at Dunhill. Instead the Russian leader was sipping champagne while smoking a cigar of Churchillian proportion. Churchill was delighted and commented that if only there was a photographer to capture the moment it would 'create an immense sensation. Everyone will say it is my influence.' Yet Churchill's influence, which had given way to that of Roosevelt at Teheran, was now almost exhausted. After just three days he and Clement Atlee returned to England to await the outcome of the General Election. Only one would return. Stalin had assured Churchill that he would win by eighty seats, indicating that the Communist dictator never could quite grasp the fickleness of democracy, for Churchill, his war efforts forgotten by a populace anxious for a new era after their exertions, was buried under a Labour landslide. Clementine Churchill tried to reassure her husband that it was a blessing in disguise. 'It is exceedingly well disguised,' replied Churchill.

FIVE

HIS MAN IN HAVANA

'The cigars of Antonio Giraudier
were the core of Churchill's collection.
Sir Winston took great delight in them.'

Sir Anthony Montague Browne

AT 3 O'CLOCK in the afternoon of Friday, 1 February 1946, the American military aircraft carrying Winston Churchill touched down on the warm tarmac of Rancho Boyeros airport, a few miles outside Havana. Fifty-one years, and two world wars, separated the young adventurer who first came under fire in Cuba and the battle-scarred, weary old man who now followed in his own footsteps. An invitation to re-visit the island had arrived while Churchill was holidaying in Miami, and he was quick to accept. As the aircraft taxied to a stop, he waved from the window and flashed the crowd his Victory sign. It was greeted by spontaneous cheers.

The official reception to greet Churchill and his

party – which included Clementine, his daughter Sarah Oliver and Frank Clark, a close friend and colonel in the Canadian army – was led by Dr Carlos Prio Socharas, the state minister for finance, and Rafael P. Gonzalez Munoz, sub-secretary of state. James L. Dodds, the British Ambassador to Cuba, was also withering under the Caribbean sun, alongside several thousand Cuban citizens, evidence of Churchill's celebrity. Once in the car Winston was photographed lighting a cigar, the first one savoured in the land of their birth for over half a century.

After a brief meeting with the Cuban President, Ramon Grau San Martin, the party was driven through crowded streets to the Hotel National, whose eucalyptus-scented gardens overlooked the Malacon, the famous ocean boulevard, to the blue sea beyond, and which was to host Churchill's first few nights. It was the hotel's manager who, hearing of Churchill's visit to Miami, had nudged the government into extending an invitation. Built in 1930, the Art Deco hotel had sheltered an array of stars including Clark Gable and Humphrey Bogart.

Churchill pulled up at the entrance and was ushered up the red carpeted steps to the presidential suite, a sumptuous set of apartments which included three bedrooms, a palatial sitting room and expansive dining room, complete with marble handbasin shaped like a Roman fountain.

It was fifteen paces from the heavy wooden door of the presidential suite, across the marble lobby to the hotel's grand hall, where at 5.30 p.m., a press conference was to be held. Churchill took twenty minutes to walk those steps, such was the scrum of admirers – the majority of whom, the following day's papers were anxious to point out, were not members of the press. 'There was disorder and great confusion, all closed round him in a circle,' said one report, while another commented, 'Winston Churchill said to the British people: "I can only offer you blood, sweat and tears"; little did he know that Cuban journalists would make him sweat more.' Finally, fumed another, 'It was not a press conference, it was a market stall.'

A market it may have been, but Churchill proved to be an entertaining auctioneer. He juggled a series of questions on foreign policy, including the arrival of British troops in Greece, to Russia's displeasure. 'If we are not there the nation will be under the Communist boot.' He refused to answer questions on the new Labour Government: 'I never criticize or talk of my government outside England.' Yet these appeared to be just preliminary rounds before the main event, the subject that linked interviewee and interviewer, the British Prime Minister and the Cuban people: the subject of cigars.

The perception that Winston Churchill used his cigars merely as a personal prop was of concern to the Cuban press, who wished to believe that his passion was sincere. So all eyes were fixed on the end of his cigar and there was relief as its red eye repeatedly winked. As one paper reported: 'He was very healthy inside a black suit and tie, without a hat, but with the unmistakable cigar in the mouth. About the cigar, many people were concerned it was a decorative one, but real smoke drew in to his lips after every answer.'

Asked about the greatness of Cuban cigars, Churchill 'took a long draw in with a delicious air' before explaining that for the moment he had no power or influence to amend the ban on importing Cuban cigars, which were still prohibited as a needless luxury during a time of economic hardship. 'Nevertheless I shall never give up promoting the Cuban cigar.'

'I, sir,' he said to one journalist, 'will be the big pro-pagandist.' To another he said: 'Cuba will always be on my lips.'

On his first evening in Cuba, Churchill dined in the

suite's private dining room with Clementine, Sarah, Frank Clark and the British Ambassador, James L. Dodds. The menu was to his satisfaction: red snapper, followed by fillet of beef and cherry dessert, all washed down by lashings of Veuve Clicquot champagne and brandy. The party's needs were looked after by a posse of five butlers who, as Churchill slept, prepared a surprise for the following morning. When he rose he immediately asked the waiter, Jorge J. Fernandez, where his cigars were. As instructed, the waiter led him into the drawing room where overnight, like Santa Claus arriving to delight a good little boy, the country's cigar manufacturers had deposited boxes and boxes of their finest wares. The highlight, from the Minister for Agriculture, was a wooden presentation box shaped like an old-fashioned treasure chest, which contained 500 cigars. Churchill, according to Fernandez, was as giddy as a schoolboy: 'He was amazed and delighted. He immediately told me to make sure no one opened the boxes and that they were to be wrapped up and shipped back to England.' Churchill shook Fernandez's hand and, unusually for a man whose breeding meant he ignored all servants, also pushed a $100 bill into his hands.

It was hardly surprising that cigars became a theme

of his trip. A few days later he was once again presented with a box of them, this time by Carmela Tiant – daughter of Pancho Tiant, the Cuban Sports Minister and president of the Havana Yacht Club, where Churchill enjoyed an official reception. Carmela Tiant wished to thank him for helping to secure a war pension after the death of her husband in the First World War. Churchill was invited to visit the tobacco plantations in Pinar Del Rio, where at this time of year the giant green leaves would have been at their most impressive. However, he declined; he may have loved the product, but had little interest in its production. Although there is some evidence that he paid a visit to the Romeo y Julieta factory, it is far from convincing. There is no listing or mention in contemporary press reports, yet there is a surviving eyewitness who insisted it took place. Jorge Jorge was a young roller of fourteen when, as he asserts, Churchill visited the plant. As Jorge rolled the longest cigars (those favoured by Winston) he was introduced to him, along with a group of other rollers. 'I could see him, but I was not so close.' A second point to support his recollection is that, following the visit, Romeo y Julieta became the first cigar company to brand this large cigar as 'Churchill's'. In a way, it was a historic handover. Until then, this particular size had been called a

'Clemenceau' after the great French Prime Minister, Georges Clemenceau. In 1918, when Churchill was Minister for Munitions, the two men had toured the front line together, puffing away and boosting morale by dispensing cigars to the troops when asked. Doubts over whether Churchill's visit to the factory ever took place grow when it is considered that there are no pictures of what would have been a considerable publicity coup. Perhaps Churchill forbade it, we do not know. What is known is that stories swirl around him and are routinely embellished. One tale (unfortunately quite false) is the claim by Gregorio Fuentes – the Cuban fisherman who, as captain of the *Pilar*, Ernest Hemingway's boat, became the inspiration for *The Old Man and the Sea* – to have hosted a cigar-smoking competition between Churchill and Hemingway. A wonderful tale and a startling image, but one which dissipates like smoke since Hemingway was in Europe at the time of Churchill's visit.

During Churchill's time in Cuba the political tension on the island continued to crackle under the surface. To the dominant right-wing government, the visit by the former Conservative Prime Minister of Great Britain was a benediction; but it was also used as a stick to beat back those who strove for greater equality and social justice. José Rivero, the deputy editor of *Diario De La Marina*, met Churchill and then wrote an editorial which stated: 'We welcome Churchill to our country and hope he does return back not only just to fill up with good Havana cigars, but also because he had a passion for Cuba. We maintain firm and fight for the same ideals of democracy and liberty, but not in the Bolshevik way.'

On Wednesday 6 February Winston and Clementine were expected to go to Trinidad, but did not do so. Churchill had found a better distraction. The party had moved from the Hotel Nacional and were now guests at the British Ambassador's residence in Jaimanitas, an affluent gardenia-scented suburb four miles from the centre of Havana. This was a short distance from the Havana Yacht Club, where Churchill met a Spanish gentleman, Antonio Giraudier, who insisted that the former Prime Minister of Great Britain deserved better than the communal facilities of even an elite private members' club. The gentleman owned a small beach house, a five-minute drive from the residence, which he put at Churchill's disposal. For the last three days of his trip, Winston rose each morning and, in blue overalls – naked underneath, according to the press – was driven by his valet to La Playita a Mirasol, as the beach was called.

An account of Churchill's routine appeared in *Diario De La Marina* on 9 February, 1946:

'Churchill takes off his overall and gets out to the water wearing a simple pair of shorts. The big back in the air and lit by the tropical sun was impressive.

'You swim well, Mr Churchill?'

'Perfectly well.'

He delights more in floating than in swimming. '20 minutes in the water. No more, no less.' Then his valet comes and gives him a towel and a cup of brandy and an enormous Havana cigar, lighting it, he again gets into the overalls and sits on the beach.

Each day, in preparation for his visit, a truckload of fresh sand was deposited on the beach and then raked smooth.

News of Churchill's daily dip swept through the nearby village and local children vied to spot him. Anna Maria Perez was fifteen when she and her brothers took their father's boat out. 'He was lying on the terrace and we could see his cigar. We shouted, "Look, look, it's Churchill," and then we saluted him and he waved back.'

While Churchill was quietly enjoying the sunshine, his doppelgänger was enjoying the roar of 30,000 people at Havana's baseball stadium. The game was stopped as an announcement was made that Mr Churchill was present. In the box a portly man was seen smoking a large cigar, making the V-sign to the crowd and signing autographs. Even when he was revealed as an imposter, the practical joke was accepted with good humour by the crowd. Before departing Cuba, Churchill visited the splendour of the American Embassy, where he was immediately presented with a frozen daiquiri in a cut-glass goblet by R. Henry Norwed, the American ambassador. Built in 1942 and equipped with a lift, wide door frames, marble floors and a manicured lawn, it was the most lavish government residence after the White House, and was designed in part as a retirement home for Roosevelt. Here Churchill felt the absence of his truculent comrade-in-arms. There was also just enough time for a day's painting in the courtyard of the Ministry for Health, whose elaborate porticoes caught his eye.

While bathing, smoking, drinking, eating and painting in Cuba, Winston Churchill had also been thinking. In his mind the great gears were grinding through the sentences and paragraphs of what would become his most controversial post-war speech. His presence on the wrong side of the Atlantic arose from an invitation to address Westminster College, a relatively obscure school in Fulton, Missouri. The attraction was that the invitation carried the personal endorsement of President Truman, who had agreed to introduce him to his home state. Churchill was a contemporary Cassandra whose dire warnings about the rise of Hitler had been ignored with devastating consequences; he was about to issue another warning, this time about Russia. The 'Iron Curtain' speech, as it would become known, was a call, not to arms but to determined diplomatic confrontation. He informed a gym hall full of students, with the wider world as his intended audience, that an 'Iron Curtain' had descended across the continent of Europe 'from Stettin in the Baltic to Trieste in the Adriatic'. He argued that peace and democracy in the post-war world could be achieved only if Britain and America, working within the framework of the United Nations, formed a Western Alliance to challenge what he saw as Russia's desire for 'the fruits of war and the indefinite expansion of their power and doctrines'. Over the next few years Churchill's speech would take concrete form with the creation of NATO, but in March 1946 he was once again ahead of the game and roundly criticized in the international press – not least, and most unsurprisingly, in *Pravda*, where Stalin accused him of 'unleashing war'.

In 1946 the Iron Curtain still seemed a long way from the warmth of Caribbean Cuba, yet within twelve years, that too would fall within its folds. And Winston Churchill's new friend, the man who presented him with a private beach and who would until Churchill's death ensure his supply of fine cigars, would have to flee.

Antonio Giraudier was a rich beer baron, despite producing what the British ambassador described as 'the only bad beer in Cuba'. Polar Beer, as it was called, slaked the thirst of millions, allowing the Spanish-born businessman to enjoy a life of comfort, if not ease. Union trouble (coupled with an excitable personality) meant that Giraudier, who despite an education at Oxford failed to graduate with the English stiff upper lip, was often in a state of stress. He and his wife lived in an elegant town house, spread over four floors, complete with an elevator; the brickwork carried a carved 'G' and the red-tile roof terrace offered views of both the towering Hotel Nacional and the blue waters of the tropical sea. The attentions of a maid, butler and driver left Giraudier time to attend – even at a distance of 4,000 miles – to his new friend, Winston Churchill. The friendship between these two men who had met at the Biltmore Havana Yacht Club, and their warm relationship of give and take – he gave, Churchill took – began with the use of the little white wooden beach house at La Playita a Mirasol. Cigars soon followed.

Giraudier decided, much as Samuel Kaplan had done during the war, to be Winston Churchill's private cigar merchant. He began by sending, three times each year, a batch of 500 'Larranaga' cigars, which Churchill had told him were unavailable in Britain. A cheque for £60 followed via the British Legation to cover duty charges. The ten packs of fifty cigars would arrive with the seasons in October, January and April, and when asked if the vitola was to his taste, Churchill replied: 'You wish to know if I like this brand. I do not think they could be bettered.' He thanked Giraudier for paying the duty, explaining that while he had the finances, he was unable to access the dollars due to restrictions in the currency exchange. He signed off: 'I wish I could spend a week of bathing on your beautiful beach.'

When Giraudier read in the *Havana Post* that Churchill was forced to cut his cigar intake to '15 per day' – a Herculean effort even by his standards – he wrote, 'Well then I must order more at once, don't you think?' There was a touch of Uriah Heep in Giraudier's devotion to a man he had met for only a few days! He wrote to Miss Sturdee, Churchill's then secretary, to ask that if ever Sir Winston should look up from puffing on his latest cigar and ponder – which was, quite frankly, unimaginable – what he, Winston Churchill, could do for Giraudier, he was to be told: 'I want him to live for many, many years and keep always one year younger. The world loves him and needs him.' There was, however, one more request: '. . . one of his pencils. Just a plain ordinary pencil. Not an expensive one.' When Miss Sturdee put the request to Churchill that his cigar supplier wished to have 'one of your used red pencils', he would not hear of it. Instead he insisted on sending not one red pencil but two blue ones which, as he pointed out, he had used on *Their Finest Hour*, the second volume of his history of the Second World War.

Winston Churchill once said: 'History will be kind to me for I intend to write it.' The post-war period, before his return to power in 1952, was spent in tremendous industry. On the political front he helped to give birth to the European Union by insisting, too early for some, that

France must work in harness with a revived Germany, and so pull the Continent together and towards peace and prosperity. On the personal front, he re-fought the Second World War, this time on paper. Hindsight not only allowed him to re-shape his actions, mask his errors and present his view of the campaign to the world, but also accomplished two further things. First, it made his fortune and secured his future and that of his children. Churchill had spend his entire life in debt; faced with a wide gulf between his income and expenditure, he preferred always to increase income rather than reduce expenditure – behaviour that tightened Clementine's nerves, which were already taut as a violin string. In 1937–38 Chartwell was placed on the market, only to be saved from sale by the deep pockets of close friends. In 1946 the house was bought for the nation and Churchill and Clementine were free to live there for the rest of their lives at a rent of £300 a year. It was a rent he could easily afford. The eventual success of *The Second World War* was staggering. The six volumes, which totalled almost two million words, were serialized in fifty publications, sold in fifteen countries and earned Churchill $2,250,000, the equivalent of $18 million today. While he believed in protecting the British state he did not care to pay taxes towards its upkeep and so, with the help of his lawyers, he created a trust which was as successful at keeping the tax man at bay as he had been at fending off the German army. The success of the books was assured by a unique deal extracted from the Cabinet Office that allowed Churchill to keep tons of official documents which by rights belonged to the British people, and under normal circumstances would have been kept secret for sixty years.*

The second purpose of writing was as a substitute for government. Instead of private secretaries, Cabinet ministers and the relentless arrival of red boxes crammed with state secrets, there were his personal secretaries, three of whom worked on rotating shifts, his 'syndicate' as he referred to the team of research assistants led by William Deakin, and the bundles of government papers to be processed, spun into golden prose and then rolled out as page proofs, on which he would repeatedly re-write and scatter cigar ash. During this time, Churchill's actual political role as Leader of the Opposition was left to Anthony Eden, his heir apparent.

Churchill's literary industry was fuelled by weak and

* The British Government secured the return of the documents in 1995 but had to pay £13.7 million to his grandson, Winston S. Churchill.

watery whiskies and his strong cigars. The man with the task of what Antonio Giraudier described as 'making the finest cigars in the world for the finest man on earth' was a middle-aged businessman called Joaquin Cuesta. He had an office and small cigar factory at number 59 Animas, just off Havana's central tree-shrouded boulevard and a couple of hundred yards from the Gran Hotel Inglaterra where Churchill first stayed in 1895. A chubby yet handsome man with dark slicked-back hair and a determined stare, he had a passion for brightly coloured ties, double-breasted suits and two-tone spats. In the late 1940s, Havana was home to hundreds of cigar factories, ranging from a few men in a back room to the giant Romeo y Julieta or H. Upmann concerns. In 1950 Cuesta asked Giraudier if he could have a portrait of Churchill. As Giraudier explained: 'Mr Cuesta is a very fine and proud man, very sentimental too and you may be sure that this matter has nothing to do at all with "advertising", it is a very personal and intimate matter which seeks no publicity whatever.' A large square photograph of a benign, smiling Churchill was duly sent and was hung above the reader's lectern in the factory's rolling room so that any weary worker could gain fresh energy and inspiration by gazing into the eyes of the man who was puffing the final result of their labours at a rate of 250 per month. (Mr Cuesta claimed that Churchill paid a visit to the factory in 1946, though there is no evidence that this took place.) In return, Cuesta had a series of sixteen photographs taken to illustrate the different stages of manufacture which each of Churchill's cigars went through. In each photograph the image of Churchill had been carefully propped up, on a worker's desk or a tobacco bale, as if to keep a careful eye on proceedings. Cuesta even had a picture taken of himself and 'Churchill' as he weaved together tobacco leaves.

Two hundred of Mr Cuesta's finest 'Coronas' were dispatched on 23 November 1951 to help Churchill celebrate his return to power in the previous month's general election. His reply was gloomy: 'To become Prime Minister of this country at the present time is nothing to be overjoyed about. We are beset by difficulties.' And so he was. Britain had lost an empire but had not yet found a role, as Dean Acheson, the American Secretary of State, stated bluntly. The country was deeply in debt, the unions had grown in strength and Churchill, now seventy-seven years old, had neither the stamina nor the interest to cope. He had printed up a new batch of stickers bearing his personal motto: 'Action This Day', but action was too often postponed until tomorrow. Domestic policy now bored Churchill, who was determined that instead his legacy should be to re-engage with Russia and so prevent the very real threat of a nuclear Armageddon; yet America, with whom it was necessary for Britain to partner, remained indifferent.

During his second term in office, Churchill chose to share the cigars he was regularly sent. Among the benefactors of his largesse was a newspaper vendor from whom he purchased a copy of the *Evening Standard* each Thursday evening as he was driven from Downing Street to Chequers, or more often to Chartwell. Lady Williams, who worked as Churchill's personal secretary from 1950 to 1955, and who accompanied him on the car journey, recalled that the Prime Minister was loyal to a particular vendor who had a pitch near Crystal Palace. She recalled: 'He was absolutely faithful to this man. We would stop the car and the detective – the security – would get out and buy the evening paper and the Prime Minister would give [the vendor] the cigar he had in his mouth. He must have had quite a collection . . . [Churchill] would roll down the window – we didn't have automatic windows – and he would just hand it over. He didn't say anything to him. He just smiled.'

While proletarian newspaper vendors warranted

a chewed and partially smoked cast-off, a former comrade-in-arms was entitled to a full untouched cigar made by Don Joaquin Cuesta. When Sir Arthur 'Bomber' Harris – the former head of Bomber Command, who had retired to South Africa – returned to Britain on a visit, he and his wife were invited to lunch at Chartwell. During the war Harris had been a compulsive cigarette smoker, consuming as many as 80 per day; yet he had since given up smoking, and as he had never smoked cigars he was unprepared for the strength of Mr Cuesta's creation. After lunch Churchill was adamant that his old colleague try one of the cigars with which he himself was so pleased, but the results were not pleasant. As Sir Arthur later noted on the label of a spice jar in which the remnants of the offending item were stored for posterity: 'Winston Churchill gave me this cigar. I was sick.' 'Bomber' Harris later described how he had retreated to the garden and vomited over the flower-beds.

In Downing Street, the valet kept a steady supply of cigars in the pantry and ensured that there was always one by the side of Churchill's bed. The Prime Minister carried, or more often had his secretary carry, a leather case that held three cigars. 'He loved Mr Giraudier's cigars – they were the best,' explained Lady Williams.

'Although sometimes if he was finding them difficult to light he would scowl and tut.' Churchill finally departed Downing Street in April 1955, but the large cases from Cuba – 'like a couple of red doors that came up to the height of your thigh', as Lady Williams recalled – continued to arrive at Chartwell.

In 1958 Antonio Giraudier extended an invitation to Winston to return to Cuba as his guest. The warm Caribbean winter, he explained, would be preferable to the chilly streets of London: 'a real paradise of continuous sunshine'. Yet the image he presented of an island where he could paint and 'smoke at ease', but where revolution was fermenting like his beer, was myopic: 'Things are quite peaceful here . . . everyone is happy and wealthy.' He believed Churchill was made of 'fine hard wood' and could easily sustain the long flight. Cooler heads prevailed, nevertheless.

Instead, Giraudier had two cases of 1934 Pol Roger champagne and bouquets of fresh flowers delivered in time for Winston and Clementine's golden wedding anniversary. He then retired to his regular suite at the Waldorf Astoria in New York, where he liked to spend each autumn, and there celebrated his seventy-second birthday on 24 September with his wife and son. Events in Cuba preyed on his mind. 'These people over there like to play tiny revolutions, which soon fade away, but make one feel uncomfortable for a while,' he explained to Churchill, before adding a final sentence: 'I believe everything will be quiet there by the end of November.'

The Cuban revolution and the collapse of the Batista government on 31 December1958, scarcely two months after Giraudier's prediction that it would 'fade away', came as a terrible shock to the elderly businessman. He returned to his home in Havana in January 1959, just as the 'war crime' trials of government officials began in the circus-like atmosphere of Havana's sports stadium, where the evidence was regularly interrupted by calls from the crowd of 'thug' and 'assassin'. Once again his concern extended only to Churchill's cigar supply. When Winston's London home in Hyde Park Gate was robbed a press report insisted, incorrectly, that his cigars were among the stolen swag. Giraudier immediately sent a telegram: 'Please cable if out of stock stop could send some airmail.' Churchill replied immediately: 'Thanks to your generosity I am still very much equipped.'

The fate of Cuba dominated the conversation when they next met on 9 May, at the elegant brownstone home of a friend in New York. The conversation began over lunch where Churchill 'ate cavier just like toast' and continued when he retired to his bedroom, where Giraudier sat in a corner chair for another hour. On Cuba, Giraudier explained: 'Whatever may come from now on, the Cuban splendour days are gone forever. It reminds me [of] the days of the French Revolution and La Bastille. God help us!'

When Giraudier returned to Havana, he found new restrictions on travel and sending money abroad. At the bank he was prohibited from sending a £50 cheque to the London Hospital for Sick Children, a practice he had maintained each June and December for many years. He was also prevented from sending money to pay the duty on Churchill's cigars, but had made arrangements with Mr Cuesta that he would cover the cost, using cash reserves he held in London, while Giraudier would repay him in Cuban coin.

For Mr Cuesta there was also the added insult of being asked by Giraudier to remove his trademark cigar bands, which bore his own beaming face, and replace them with plain bands of red and gold. As Giraudier explained in a letter to Doreen Pugh, Churchill's secretary: 'Of course he is proud of his trade mark and the high quality he makes for Sir Winston, but I don't like these rings and I don't think Sir Winston likes them, because he asked me at lunchtime when he got his cigar out of the case – who is that man?!!'

Churchill would have liked Mr Cuesta's alternative band even less. For in Cuba Cuesta's cigars now carried the imprimatur of his most famous customer, an image of Churchill in silhouette but recognizable by his top hat and a cigar.

Giraudier also took time during the lunch to talk of his son Tony, a poet, painter and novelist whose latest book of poems his father presented to Churchill, saying, 'He would rather have just one word from you, than all the good writing he has had from French, Italian, Spanish and American critics.' Churchill wrote back and praised his work as: 'very interesting'.

Restrictions on travel and trade were tightened further by July 1959. Foreign currency was permissible only for the purchase of raw materials and machinery. To finance a trip abroad any individual was permitted $500 on the first occasion, with all subsequent trips restricted to $50. 'As you can see this will not take you very far,' wrote Giraudier to Churchill, and continued:

> Up to the present time I have been lucky because Mr Cuesta (the man who makes the special cigars for Sir Winston) has some money in the bank in London and he has been sending you the cheques since January asking his bank in London to send them to you. He is now running short of it and the government has discovered that he has money in London and also in the U.S.A for his business and now he has to declare it and pay taxes on it.

All gifts of champagne, hams, flowers and stockings for the secretaries would now have to cease. 'You do not know how deeply I regret it.' Cigars would still be sent, but in a reduced quantity. At their earlier meeting in New York Churchill had said he could now manage only five cigars each day, so all subsequent orders were cut by half. The message was passed on to Churchill, who was then cruising in the Mediterranean.

Doreen Pugh wrote a note to Anthony Montague Browne, who had met and admired Giraudier, asking if she should ask Giraudier to stop sending the cigars: 'I will say that of course we completely understand and do not expect any cigar duty or anything else, and are extremely grateful for all his kindness to us in the past etc, etc. But should Sir Winston tell him not to bother about sending cigars if it is in any way difficult? And should we offer to help in any way with funds?'

Despite the new wealth generated by his history of the Second World War, Churchill still enjoyed his free cigars; while explaining that he need not continue to send them, he did not explicitly instruct Giraudier not to do so. He wrote on 17 August: 'You have been so very generous to me for many years, and your gifts have been a source of great pleasure both to myself and to my family. I do trust that you will not continue to send cigars if this puts you in any difficulty. Of course I can deal with the duty in Great Britain, but I realize that other problems may well present themselves for you.'

However, Giraudier insisted that the cigars would continue to come. 'You will have them all the time . . . they are a Cuban product, the only trouble is in foreign currency.'

In September Giraudier once again returned to the Waldorf Astoria. He had spent the past few weeks in America, reorganizing his business affairs so that they would provide 'some more protection' from the coming storm. In New York, free from the eye of the government censor or spy, he wrote a gloomy critique on his country: 'Things in Cuba do not look well at all. In fact, they get worst [*sic*] every day. That man is out of his mind. His only thought: capital destruction. Communism, but under different names such as cubanism, humanism etc., but they are sowing the seeds of socialism.'

He went on to explain that all government schools had been issued with new schoolbooks, detailing the history of communism, and commented: 'Economically, I don't think Cuba can hold for more than two or three years. This is also the general opinion here in the USA. Everybody here, and in Cuba, and also in other parts of the world, is wondering if England will give Castro the jet bombers he is asking for – we all know that if he gets them, he will soon start to use them in combined action with his Venezuelan brothers to hit Santo Domingo first and create all kinds of troubles which are in his insane mind. We all hope England will think it over.'

He closed the letter by saying: 'We are all well at the present time and we hope for a better future, but we can see no lights of help in our horizon.'

The reply from Chartwell, written by Montague Browne, made no mention of Cuba's troubles. As Browne explained in a note to Churchill: 'It would clearly embarrass him if one made any mention of the substance of his letter, since I have no doubt that the Cuban authorities are very likely to open letters received from abroad.' So instead Giraudier learned only of Churchill planting a tree at Churchill College, Cambridge, and that he listened to songs at Harrow. There was no stirring speech, no urge to 'Keep Buggering On'.

There was, however, an uplifting Christmas present, a finely bound copy of *Churchill: The Walk With Destiny*, a fawning biography, to which each member of the Chartwell staff had signed their names, and an extended message of gratitude for all Giraudier's presents of Christmases past. It was, he said, 'the most wonderful Christmas present'.

In the months after the Cuban revolution Fidel Castro's cigar was as much a part of his swaggering image as the pistol around his waist and the green army fatigues. He was, in fact, the first Cuban president to smoke cigars. During the 1940s and 1950s President Prio smoked cigarettes, while both Battista and Dr Grau were non-smokers. Even Che Guevara – who as an asthmatic

Argentine doctor had been vigorously opposed to cigars, preferring instead the pipe – initially recommended it as the ideal smoking implement for the guerrilla fighter, eventually succumbing to the allure of a Havana once he landed on the island. Like Churchill, Fidel Castro enjoyed smoking other people's cigars. Unlike Churchill (who at least waited until they were presented to him) Castro would bully cigars from the top pockets of sub-ordinates. Guillermo Cabrera Infante, the Cuban writer, explained how Castro smoked three of his four cigars before hinting heavily that he wished to apprehend the fourth, which Infante was then obligated to hand over. There were other differences in their smoking habits. While Churchill was oblivious to the servants or staff who cleared away his ashtray , Castro was guilt-ridden, once writing in jail: 'There is nothing more agreeable than having a place where one can throw on the floor as many cigar butts as one pleases, without the sub-concious fear of a maid who is waiting like a sentinel to place an ashtray where the ashes are going to fall.'

Cigars have held a unique place in political life. Thomas Riley Marshall, the Vice-President under Woodrow Wilson, commented of America in the 1920s: 'What this country needs is a really good five cent cigar.' In Cuba, the relationship between politics and tobacco was even closer, as Dr Fernando Ortiz wrote in *Cuba Counterpoint*: 'He who governs Cuba must rule over Havanas', and Fidel Castro's rule was to be supreme. In Cuba in the 1950s, there were almost 1,000 small cigar factories employing from a handful to a few dozen staff, while the number of large-scale factories had dropped from seventy in 1910 to just twenty. On 15 September 1960, Castro ordered the nationalization of the cigar industry. Armed soldiers arrived at the gates of the tobacco plantations, while in Havana the factory offices were taken over and their safes sealed, and the profits claimed in the name of the revolution. Owners were offered new positions as mere managers.

By May 1960 the political climate so chilled Giraudier that he prepared to leave. A concern was what to do with his complete collection of Churchill's works and two of his oil paintings. On 4 May Giraudier wrote to Chartwell to ask if the British Ambassador would agree to store his collection at the Embassy. Anthony Montague Browne then wrote to H.S. Marchant, who had only just arrived on the island, requesting that he offer Giraudier any assistance. But Marchant was concerned about the implications. 'Having experienced this sort of thing in Romania, only to find myself accused, amongst other crimes of aiding "enemies of the people's government" to avoid taxation etc. etc., I am anxious not to repeat at any rate this particular mistake.' He said, however, that he would do 'my very best to help his friend'.

Fortunately, while waiting for a reply, Giraudier had found shelter for his collection in the Spanish Embassy.

In May 1960 Fidel Castro sent Winston Churchill a box of cigars via Tito Arias, the Panamanian revolutionary, who had been introduced to the former Prime Minister by Aristotle Onassis. Churchill, recalled his grandson, Winston S. Churchill, was very keen to accept this surprise bounty. Anthony Montague Browne insisted that this was impossible and that, as Castro was a revolutionary with blood on his hands, the cigars should be returned. As he explained in a note to the British Ambassador to Cuba: 'For your most private information . . . I managed to get the box returned without hurting anybody's feelings.' As his grandson remembered: 'My grandfather was very chewed up about seeing these splendid cigars going back.' The exact make of those particular cigars is unknown; however, the following year Castro was to employ Eduardo Rivera Irizarri, a friend of his bodyguard and an experienced roller, to prepare his own personal supply, safe from any potentially lethal interference from the CIA.

So pleased was Castro by Irizarri's elegantly shaped and sweet-smoking cigars that he appointed him director of the El Laguito factory in Havana, set up to train female rollers but which as a sideline produced the cigars that Castro personally gave as gifts. These cigars, which Castro insists were delivered annually to Winston Churchill's London address, were the forerunners of the Cohiba, considered the world's finest cigar, created in 1966 and originally designed as a diplomatic gift to governments.

For Giraudier, circumstances had grown intolerable. The Polar Beer Brewery was to be collectivized and pulled into government hands. His income was reduced to a few thousand pesos a month and, by the summer's end, he had been forced to sell property, land and bonds which he converted into dollars at a deplorable rate of 350 pesos to the dollar.

In September Giraudier, his wife and their son, Tony, decided to leave. While Churchill's paintings and books were safely stored at the Spanish Embassy, much of the contents of the family's town house in Vedado was donated to the Catholic Church and the keys left with the family maid, Candaida Rodriguez, who lived on the top floor and agreed to wait for their return. She died in 1988, still waiting.

The family travelled to Miami and then on to New York City, where Giraudier wrote to Churchill on 10 October: 'We are so happy to feel that we are in this free country and we can talk and write without fear. It was terrible in Cuba. Every day we were afraid that someone would accuse us to be against the communist government, which would mean immediate action against us all.' In another letter he wrote: 'They have taken everything from us. We have nothing left in Cuba.'

The family, he said, would stay in New York until November, when they would return to Miami 'to the warm weather' and there make plans for 'staying out of Cuba – only God knows how long'. Castro, he insisted, was 'nothing but a part of [the] Soviet Union and their target is the United States'. In the same note he predicted the Cuban missile crisis of 1962: 'The United States will have a new president and perhaps a new government. If they take any action against Cuba then the Soviets might get in too – then no one can foresee the end.' Churchill received the letter while at the Hotel de Paris in Monte Carlo and replied on 20 October: 'We are all distressed that you and your family should be going through this worrying and difficult time, and my thoughts are with you.' He explained that the gifts of cigars were no longer necessary: 'I do feel that now you are no longer in Cuba you should not continue to send me cigars, as you have done so generously for a long time. I know that it cannot be easy for you to make these arrangements and I shall fully understand if you no longer do so.'

Yet he had underestimated Giraudier's tenacity and his desire to hold on to his role as supplier of cigars to 'the greatest man the world has ever had'.

Before leaving Cuba Giraudier had asked Cuesta to continue the regular shipments, and had left money to pay for them with his lawyer. The last batch left in November. It was no longer possible to write directly to Cuesta in Havana, as all mail from Miami was opened.

Giraudier had now settled in Coconut Row in Palm Beach, where the people were 'nice and distinguished, not much like in Miami'. When he heard that Churchill was embarking on a cruise of the West Indies on the *Christina*, Aristotle Onassis's yacht, he sent a case of Fremicourt brandy to steady his sea-legs. The itinerary did not include a call in Florida, but weather forced the boat to stop, allowing Giraudier and Churchill to meet once again. The two men enjoyed lunch on board the *Christina* in April. 'Mr Onassis and his sister were also so very kind,' wrote Giraudier. Yet it was now time for him to call in a favour. Under the current regulations, he and his wife were permitted to stay in America only after first securing a temporary resident's permit which involved regularly leaving the country to re-apply. The most accessible spot being Nassau in the Bahamas, Giraudier asked if Churchill could help smooth the path clear.

Anthony Montague Browne then wrote to the British authorities there to ask: 'Sir Winston would not of course wish to ask the authorities to do anything improper, but to the best of our knowledge Mr Giraudier is and always has been entirely respectable and is not engaged in émigré politics.'

The British Consul in the Bahamas did indeed speak with the American Consul, who advised that Giraudier and his wife would be considered for permanent entry visas. As Montague Browne wrote back on 29 May 1961: 'It is a little difficult for us to intervene with the American authorities, as I am sure you will understand, but I have been told privately that the American Consul-General in Nassau "is prepared to consider an application for visas", which I have little doubt means a favourable answer.'

On 10 July Giraudier decided to travel to Nassau for a period of six months, but first they travelled to

Montreal, where he celebrated his seventy-fifth birth-day. By September 1961 the Cuban cigars from Havana had stopped. 'Sir Winston has derived great enjoyment over many years from the fine cigars you have sent him in such numbers, and he is deeply grateful to you, which I think you know.'

The Giraudiers arrived at the Nassau Beach Hotel on 30 September and wrote to thank Churchill for his assistance in helping them gain access 'to this piece of heaven' where they planned to become permanent residents. The couple had initially experienced some resistance at the customs, but were waved through when Mrs Giraudier produced a signed photograph of Churchill from her handbag. As Giraudier said: 'It worked just like a magic key.' In November he asked Churchill if he would write a letter of reference saying '. . . that you believe we would make very nice residents.' As he explained: 'I would appreciate receiving this favour from you . . . because I must tell you that we have had all the doors open wide, whenever we have mentioned your name.' As a result of Churchill's assistance, Giraudier was promptly issued with a four-year residency permit and praised for his contacts.

The news that cigars were no longer being sent from Havana to Chartwell upset Giraudier, who feared for the fate of Joaquin Cuesta. He had been unable to write directly to him for fear of 'getting him into trouble'. In Nassau he had met a purser on the SS *Florida*, which used to sail between Havana and Miami and now serviced Nassau–Miami. Giraudier had promised to speak with a friend who was a pilot with Pan-America flying into Havana, and who undertook to try to discover Cuesta's location. Giraudier was later to ask Churchill's secretary, Miss Pugh, to write to Cuesta's address in Animas, even explaining how the letter should be composed. However, Churchill felt this was not proper; as it was explained to Giraudier: 'He has enjoyed your cigars for such a long time, and he would prefer not to trouble Mr Cuesta. He may be in difficulties over the matter, and Sir Winston does not want to risk embarrassing him.' Yet Giraudier had not yet given up: 'I do have hopes that I can furnish Sir Winston with his cigars again – I don't know how, but I will.'

On 12 June Giraudier discovered that Joaquin Cuesta was alive 'somewhere in Miami' and that his two sons were rolling cigars in Tampa. Previous cables and enquiries by cigar importers had been met by silence. 'I really have been very much upset for these two last years, as nobody has been able to tell me if he was dead or alive.'

Yet Giraudier had already found an alternative supplier, Cuban brothers based in Miami, Camacho Cigars Inc., who had obtained a stock of Cuban tobacco and had put their best men on the task of making fifty cigars for Churchill at a cost of just $62, the equivalent of £20.

The arrival of the cigars on 4 July could not have been better timed. Montague Browne took them straight to hospital, where Churchill was recovering after breaking his hip while holidaying in Monte Carlo. As he wrote on 24 July: 'I find that Sir Winston has tried both the green and the mature cigars, and is enjoying them both very much. If anything, he has a slight preference for the green leaf.'

Giraudier wrote back:

About Cigars: I was so happy when you told me that he likes them. These cigars were made for him by two brothers who are in Miami and they were able to bring with them leaves and also the Colorado Claro and they are making some fine cigars for some of the Cubans who are here and in Miami but of course, it is a small business, nothing like what they had in Havana, they have not got enough good tobacco, but they have put aside for me some of the very best for Sir Winston and as you say that he

likes them both, they are now making 75 cigars of
the green leaf and 25 cigars of the Colorado Claro
(light red leaf) – it will take perhaps two more
weeks, before they have to go to the man who rolls
them before they have been properly cured. By the
end of this month or before, you will have 100 cigars
to offer him again! And we shall keep on doing so
as long as the material is available.

Once again, the cigars were sent by sea to lengthen the
curing process. Giraudier's main concern was that they
would be of an inferior quality compared with the
Havanas crafted by Cuesta's hands, so he asked Montague Browne to inspect them carefully before passing
them on to Churchill. Giraudier himself began inspecting the cigars before dispatch and reported that the
'workmanship is not as perfect as it was with Cuesta',
who rejected 200 out of every 1,000 cigars as unaccept-
able. 'I know that no better cigars can be had here now,
but I don't know if they will be good enough for Sir Winston.'

On 12 December he was assured that they were
highly acceptable. 'I am most grateful to you for sending me more of those excellent cigars,' wrote Churchill.

Winston enjoyed Giraudier's cigars, but did not abandon his long relationship with Robert Lewis, which by 1959 had passed from the hands of Fred Croley to his son John. Their relationship had been a testing but ultimately loving one, which began shortly before the outbreak of war and continued once peace had been restored. As an enlisted man John Croley had travelled through Egypt, Malta and North Africa before returning to Britain in 1944 to train for a commission. He returned to the cigar shop, unannounced. His father informed him that his eldest sister, Joan, and her husband, George, were dying of tuberculosis, the disease that had already claimed their infant son. When John reached Portsmouth, Joan said: 'Thank God you've come. Now I can die in peace,' as she did the following day. During his military service John Croley had followed the development of radar, and also worked briefly (though saw no action) with Colonel Stirling's SAS. After completing officer training in Kent and gaining a commission, he was seconded to the King's Own in northern Italy, where his duties involved looking after surrendered enemy personnel. At one point he had to rescue a group of Italian prisoners-of-war from a mafia businessman who had 'bought' fifty of them from his predecessor. When John Croley eventually returned home in 1947 with an Italian wife, Lisl, he bridled under the role of trainee to his father where previously he had been a lieutenant commanding a troop of men.

While it was clear that Fred Croley had performed a miracle in squeezing the company through the war intact, it was also clear that Robert Lewis could not continue without diversifying. As Fred gritted his teeth, John introduced luxury goods such as leather pipe tobacco pouches, hand-made cigarette lighters and, later, cocktail glasses to cater for the post-war trend for DIY Singapore Slings. Surprisingly it was glasswear that led, by a circuitous route, to the store's largest ever single order of cigars. One day a gentleman enquired about purchasing a solitary glass from an exceedingly expensive pack of six finely cut crystal goblets. When the customer explained that he was en route to Hyde Park for an impromptu picnic, John fetched a glass from upstairs and lent it to him. It transpired that the gentleman was a senior army officer who then encouraged his fellow officers to frequent Robert Lewis; one of them placed an order for cigars worth £49,500.

Winston Churchill would never be so ambitious, but after the death of Fred Croley in 1959, John Croley took to visiting Chartwell with the latest batch of cigars. He recalled: 'I had the pleasure of seeing him many, many times in bed in the morning with papers and cigar ash all around him. There is a very funny incident in the summer before he died. When I was showing him a box of Romeo y Julieta when his secretary, Miss Pugh, unfortunately dropped the box on the floor, then you heard the Churchill roar and I was left not knowing quite what to do. I brought the box back and replaced it.' Churchill greatly admired Romeo y Julieta, elevating it above many others. His respect for this cigar is illustrated in a letter sent to the tobacconist on 8 October 1963, in which his secretary requests that a box of twenty-five cigars be sent to his grandson. The letter states that the cigars be of 'good quality, but not quite as good as the Romeo & Julieta'.

Unlike John Croley, Antonio Giraudier – like so many distant friends – was shielded from the true extent of Winston Churchill's decline. Letters beseeching Churchill to visit Palm Beach, and come to live for 'many, many years in the best of health' at a new house Giraudier was making plans to purchase for him, were politely but firmly declined with the explanation that 'it is difficult for Sir Winston to travel so far at the present time'. In actual fact, it was only with difficulty that Churchill could walk from one room to another. He was prohibited by his doctors from returning to Chartwell and in his last few years the stairs at 28 Hyde Park Gate proved too much, so a new bedroom was prepared downstairs in Montague Browne's old office. In 1963 he was both pressured and persuaded to step down as an MP by his family; this was much to the relief of his constituency, who no longer wished to have a relic, however great his past, representing – or, in fact, incapable of representing – their present. Any form of work, however simple, was now beyond his capability. As he said to Clementine: 'I eats well, and I drinks well and I sleeps well, but when I sees a job of work, I comes all over a-tremble.' This enforced retirement severed the remaining cable that had anchored him to life. He had once told Lord Moran: 'I think I shall die quickly once I retire. There would be no purpose in living when there is nothing to do.' As Montague Browne memorably described them, these were 'rare sparks in a fire that had already burnt grey'.

Churchill's life had been reduced to visits from the few people who could inspire his interest; friends such as Jock Colville and Ari Onassis. His deafness, memory lapses and drifting concentration made conversation almost impossible. Although still able to read the occasional novel, he spent most days lost in a mist of melancholy that obscured his great achievements and left only his failures on view. 'Demons seem to whisper things to him,' said Violet Bonham Carter. On one occasion, Anthony Montague Browne tried to clear the fog by asking him how he could be so sad, having achieved so much: the Nobel prize for literature, a great body of historical work and his greatest achievement, the salvation of Britain that still generated, twenty years on, the adoration of his countrymen. As Browne stated, he was even cheered in Germany. But Churchill could not be consoled. His goal had always exceeded his grasp: that of a powerful British Empire in a peaceful world.

'What you say is historically correct,' said Winston. 'I have worked hard all my life, and I have achieved a great deal – in the end to achieve nothing.'

A cigar, so it is said, can be a 'sad man's consolation'. Churchill was consoled by his cigars up until the very end of his life, to the consternation and perpetual worry of Clementine. Her fear, so common to the carers of any elderly person who smokes, was that her husband would set himself alight. And on occasion he did.

The wife of Montague Browne, who worked as an assistant to Clementine, was repeatedly asked to 'check on Winston' as he puffed away in bed. As Shelagh recalled: 'On one occasion I walked in just as the flames began to creep up the newspaper he was holding. Ash had dropped and set it alight, and he was oblivious, quite oblivious.' On 30 November 1964, at Hyde Park Gate, he sat silently puffing and endured, as others enjoyed, his ninetieth birthday party. As Mary Soames recalled: 'Although he beamed at us all, we all gathered round him and one felt he was glad to have us there, in our hearts we knew the end could not be far off.'

Churchill placed his final cigar order with Robert Lewis on 23 December 1964. It consisted of 25 Piramidas and 25 Alergo Reala, at a total cost of £20 and 12 pence. According to Montague Browne, he smoked his last cigar on the evening of 9 January 1965. After puffing softly, the cigar faded between his lips, and by the time it was placed in the bedside ashtray it was already quite dead. The constant companion of seventy-five years, forever six inches ahead of the most remarkable man of the twentieth century, had – as good friends do – continued to lead the way.

In the dark hours between the 9th and the 10th of January, Winston Churchill suffered a massive stroke.

He never regained consciousness and died two weeks later on 24 January 1965, exactly seventy years to the day since the death of his father, for whom he swore never to smoke.

SIX

THE ASHES

'I thought: "I'm going to get that cigar".
So when he left it, I pulled it out of the grate,
carried it up to my room and put it in a box."

Elizabeth Nel, Winston Churchill's secretary

LORD MORAN, WINSTON CHURCHILL'S personal physician, best captured the occasion of his patient's burial at Bladon Churchyard: 'And in a country churchyard, in the stillness of a winter evening, in the presence of his family and a few friends, Winston Churchill was committed to the English earth, which in his finest hour he had held inviolate.' As the coffin was lowered six feet down, plans were already being drawn up for the erection of statues as towering as his reputation.

Today, in London, he stares down from a plinth in Parliament Square, dressed in overcoat and leaning heavily on a cane, his eyes cast over the Houses of Parliament. A second statue, inside Parliament, keeps a watchful eye on generations of new members. In Bond Street, on a park bench, he shares a joke with Franklin Roosevelt. In Paris, Strasbourg, Washington D.C. and in Kansas City there too are busts and statues, but only in a little town in Australia is there a suitably dramatic tribute to his cigar habit, and even then its symbolism came about by accident.

Known simply as 'The Big Cigar', it stands 101 feet 4 inches tall in the civic square of the town of Churchill, in the province of Victoria. The structure, made of galvanized steel and coated in gold anodized perforated aluminium sheeting, is now a curious tourist attraction which competes on the continent with 'The Big Banana' in Coffs Harbour, in New South Wales, 'The Big Captain Cook' in Cairns, 'The Big Crocodile' in Wyndham and 'The Big Cigarette' in Myrtleford. There is also a 'Big Koala', 'Big Fruit Bowl' and 'Big Golden Guitar' scattered across the country.

A town called Churchill with a giant cigar at its centre would be an act of deliberate design, or so one would be forgiven for thinking, especially since Australia has shown such an affection for Churchill, one which quite dwarfs the ex-Prime Minister's reciprocal feelings. In fact, Winston Churchill could be accused of having treated Australia quite shabbily. After all, he was the principal architect of the Gallipoli campaign which cost the lives of 6,000 Australian troops. During the Second World War he cast doubt on their power of perseverance over Tobruk and the fall of Singapore, and was dismissive of the Australian Government – particularly under Robert Menzies – and their attempts to influence policy. Yet Australia took these blows on the chin, continued to hold him to their heart and, following his death, reached swiftly and deeply into their pockets to raise $2.3 million in a single day to set up the Winston Churchill Memorial Trust, which continues to administer travelling fellowships to young Australians.

Throughout Australia over 150 streets and thoroughfares were named after Churchill, though the decision to saddle a new town in Victoria with the title would prove controversial. The town, a satellite community for the Hazelwood Power Plant in the La Trobe Valley, was intended to be called Hazelwood after the daughter of an early settler, a girl named Hazel; unfortunately this clashed with another neighbouring town, and the postmaster insisted that such confusion would be intolerable. Despite this, a 'Don't Change to Churchill' campaign was set up by a local RAAF veteran by the appropriate name of Tom Lawless, which was then dismissed as 'the greatest possible insult to the name of a great wartime leader' by the State Housing Minister. The State Cabinet had to visit the valley in an attempt to placate the locals, and though the decision was passed by six votes to five, not everyone was convinced. The sign was riddled with gunshots soon after its erection.

At first, 'The Big Cigar' was equally unpopular. What was designed by the Housing Commission as a giant spire to 'inspire' the residents of the new town was unwelcome. Residents would have preferred a swimming pool and grudged the $30,000 cost. Unveiled on 21 December 1967, it was re-christened 'The Big Cigar' three weeks later when, on 10 January 1968, the Latrobe Valley Express printed a cartoon depicting it as a cigar wrapped with a band on which appeared the letter 'V' for victory. Its new identity was sealed and so, less than three years after the death of Winston Churchill, a 101-foot monument, taller than any of his own statues, was now in place, dedicated – at least in the minds of residents and visitors, if not its original designer – to his cigar.

'The Big Cigar' was true to life in that it frequently went out. Equipped with 1,000-watt floodlights to give the cigar a warm glow, the tip proved attractive to nesting birds which played havoc with the lighting system. In 1999 a new lighting system was installed, so after thirty years it remains a beacon to Churchill's passion.

So, in the Australian outback Churchill's Cigar was towering up towards the stars, while on the London stage the stars were peering down at Churchill's Cigar. In March 1969, fifteen months after the erection in Australia, Joe Orton's controversial play *What the Butler Saw* opened at the Queen's Theatre in London. Sigmund Freud, an inveterate cigar smoker who puffed through a box each day, was once chastized for smoking a cigar on the grounds that it was an obvious phallic symbol. He famously replied: 'Sometimes a cigar is just a cigar.' In Orton's play a cigar was most certainly not just a cigar. At the climax of the farce, Orton's original plan was to have the former Prime Minister's penis in a box, having been broken off a statue. The script reads:

Rance looks inside the box.
Rance (with admiration): 'How much more inspiring if, in those dark days, we'd seen what we see now. Instead we had to be content with a cigar – the symbol falling far short, as we realize, of the object itself.'
Geraldine looks inside the box.

Geraldine: 'But it is a cigar!'
Rance: 'Ah, the illusions of youth!'

Given Churchill's appetite for exceedingly large cigars, Joe Orton attempted to convince his producer, Oscar Lewenstein, that the lines were a compliment rather than a cause of offence. 'What am I saying about Churchill, though?' asked the playwright. 'You're saying he had a big prick,' said Lewenstein. Orton then replied, 'That isn't libel, surely, I wouldn't sue anybody for saying I had a big prick. No man would. In fact I might pay them to do that.'

Sir Ralph Richardson, the august patrician actor, would have none of it and the penis was turned into a cigar for the actual production. However, this act failed to save him from the contempt of old ladies, whom Stanley Baxter (who was among the cast) described as: '. . . not merely tearing up their programmes, but jumping up and down on them out of sheer hatred.'

Joe Orton did not live to see the production, being killed by his lover's hand in September 1967. It is interesting to speculate with what epithets Churchill might have greeted him at the Pearly Gates.

Full-length cigars, half-smoked stubs, struck matches and a variety of cigar cases and humidors owned by Churchill have been treasured, or reluctantly sold, since his death. In the Churchill Museum, which opened in January 2005 next to the Cabinet War Rooms in London, a sixty-year-old cigar sits under glass. A close inspection reveals that it is one of the few remaining from the batches sent by Samuel Kaplan and bears the name 'Winston Churchill' on the paper band. The cigar was donated by Elizabeth Nel, who was one of Churchill's team of secretaries during the Second World War and regularly typed or took shorthand in a room filled with smoke. She recalled:

> I grew quite addicted to the smell of the smoke. You see he would light up his cigar and have some puffs but then his mind was always on his work, always on his work, and he would forget to puff and then he would have to re-light. The cigar was always going out. He always had a big, big box of matches. This box had big matches in it and he would strike it up and there would be a big flame and the flame always went up and down. He would puff until it

was lit and then flick his wrist to put out the match. That happened many times in the day. He smoked them half way and when he was finished with it he would whip round and throw it into the fireplace.

I didn't mind the smell. War was different. Everything went to the war. In my case and those who worked in the same capacity as me, everything was for Mr Churchill. One's life was utterly devoted to doing one's best not to annoy him, not to cause him to waste time. He couldn't bear to waste time. I remember once he said to Mr [Anthony] Eden: 'This lady is quick and intelligent and so much time is saved.' That was his point. Everything was to save time, because there was so much that he wanted to do. And that he had to do, and there was never time to do it all.

Elizabeth's memory of taking her 'souvenir' remains fresh:

It must have been a few Days before VE day. We were at Chequers and Mr Churchill was having his afternoon rest when we got the call from No. 10 which one always took down verbatim, and it was a telegram from General Alexander who was the commander-in-chief of Bat Sic; it was to say that he had had a complete surrender of all the German forces in Italy. An unconditional surrender. So I rushed upstairs to his bedroom thinking that he would be terribly pleased about this. He was sitting up in bed reading. And he just read the note and put it aside and didn't say anything. I was so disappointed.

Then when he came downstairs he was as happy as a schoolboy. He got on the telephone to No 10. He had just lit up a cigar and he took some puffs and then when he got on the line, he just took it out of his mouth and threw it in the grate of the fireplace. So I thought to myself, I never keep mementos of this kind, I felt it wouldn't be right, but I thought I'm going to get that cigar. So when he left I took it, I pulled it out of the grate, carried it up to my room and put it in a box.

I kept it carefully in this nice long box which I used to keep jewellery in. I kept it for years, and years and years. Occasionally I might show it to a friend who might be interested in it. One friend said, 'Shall I light it up and then I can have a puff?' I said, 'Aargh! Put it down.'

After the war Nel emigrated to South Africa with her husband, and the cigar made occasional trips from its box to her daughter's school. As her daughter recalled: 'Looking at the cigar, it did, in a strange way, give us a better knowledge of the great man. It was a thrilling reaction.'

According to Elizabeth Nel, the cigar bands that bore Churchill's name were particularly popular: 'I don't think there were many souvenir hunters in those days, but everything was lying on the desk and on the floor and people would pick them up and take them. It was not their intention to come in and try to find something to take, they just made a good souvenir.'

Elizabeth Nel secured both cigar and band, but Harry Newcombe – one of Britain's last surviving veterans of the Great War – secured only the band, which he treasured for decades. A private in the Sussex Regiment, Newcombe served with the Army of Occupation in Germany in 1919. During the Second World War he worked as a waiter on the Great Western Railway and, one evening, served Churchill his supper. His promptness in fetching an evidently thirsty Prime Minister his Scotch and soda was rewarded by the gift of the cigar band – once again from Kaplan's personalized batch. He looked after his souvenir for over thirty years until it was tragically lost. In 2005, Harry Newcombe, aged 105, was resident in a nursing home, his memories of that day sadly lost to dementia.

Yet it was not only individuals but tobacconists who were anxious to preserve Churchill's smoke. In 1946, G. de Graaff, an established tobacconist in The Hague, was asked to provide cigars for a lunch given by Queen Wilhelmina for Winston Churchill. A box was provided and, according to a legal document drawn up by Mr de Graaff's solicitor, Churchill began to smoke one before lunch was served. Queen Wilhelmina found smoking during lunch distasteful and even Churchill, liberator of her nation, was obliged to comply. The cigar was laid down and never picked up again, except when cleared away by Churchill's butler, who duly passed it on to one of the Queen's footmen – it is not known if it was carried on a velvet pillow – who in turn presented it to Mr de Graaff. He then had it framed, alongside one full cigar from the box sent along to the lunch. The long cinnamon-coloured cigars, described by one visitor to the shop as 'dry as old turds', are in a glass box, sealed with red wax, to which a copper plate is attached that reads: '1946, Sir Winston Churchill's cigar'. In London, the remnants of the cursed cigar that made 'Bomber' Harris sick, and which is still stored in the spice jar into which he placed it, can be inspected at Tom Tom, a cigar emporium owned by his grandson.

The growth of Churchilliana – products incorporating his appearance – was already strong before his death, but it subsequently rocketed. The cigar manufacturer Mercator Vander Elst produced a set of twenty-four cigar bands, each bearing Churchill's head with a different style of headgear, from sailor's cap to top hat, from an ostrich-plumed naval affair which would befit Nelson to his bare bald pate. Freed from the threat of legal action which would undoubtedly have rained down during Churchill's life, cigar manufacturers began to emblazon his face on bands and boxes in an attempt to fuse his face to their wares. Confectioners too leapt into the fray, with one company from the Netherlands producing a 12-inch-long chocolate cigar which, until fairly recently, was sold in British Home Stores. In 1974, the centenary of Winston's birth, Asprey, the elegant London jewellers, misfired by producing a rosewood and cedar-lined cigarette box bearing his face which, knowing of Churchill's own distaste for cigarettes, should have been curled in disgust.

However, his face would no doubt beam with surprise at the news that his cigars have become the most expensive in the world. In the last decade cigars that have been part of his collection, or had passed his lips, have sold at auction for thousands of pounds. In April 1996 Christie's sold two of Don Joaquin Cuesta's cigars, tucked in an 18-carat gold cigar case, for £3,785. The following year Sotheby's sold another cigar case, one carried by Churchill in the trenches of the First World War, for £4,830. In 1998 Sotheby's sold the 9-carat gold cigar case, made by Cartier, which commemorated six cruises Churchill had taken on the *Christina* with Aristotle Onassis, who presented it to him on his eighty-sixth birthday; the final bid was £43,300. Other sales have included a cigar box stamped Romeo y Julieta 'Made in Cuba' and given by Churchill to Brendan Bracken, the Minister of Information, which sold in April 2005 for £2,600. Marvin Shanken, the publisher of *Cigar Aficionado*, was famous for spending £250,000 on JFK's humidor; furthermore, he quietly paid an unknown sum for one of Winston Churchill's humidors which he is said to prefer.

The most expensive single cigar, meanwhile, was a half-smoked stub that Churchill tapped out in the studio of Oscar Nemon, the London sculptor, when he posed in the 1950s. When sold in December 2002, the bidding reached £2,270.

And so the story of Churchill's cigar draws to a close. The Prime Minister's name is on the bands of over one hundred different cigar brands, as well as being declared on the billboards of tobacconists and cigar lounges in countries around the world. Yet while Churchill could lead the way and smoke wherever he sat, sadly the cigar has become unpopular. The perfect example of this trend to banish what he cherished took place in August 2006 in Edinburgh, where recently introduced anti-smoking legislation prevented actors performing in the Edinburgh Festival and Fringe from lighting up on stage. The most prominent casualty was Winston Churchill himself, as portrayed by Mel Smith in a play called *Allegiance* written by the Irish author Mary Kenny, which detailed the relationship between Churchill and Michael Collins. Smith, who is himself a cigar smoker, was incensed, insisting that the ban would have delighted Adolf Hitler and promising to fight back and accept a £50 fine. However the venue, fearful of losing its licence, urged him to capitulate. And so, at each performance, Churchill's cigar was still.

In England and Wales, as in Italy, Ireland and sundry American states, the cigar smoker has been withdrawn from restaurants and bars, gently ushered away with the long hand of the law clasping him firmly by the elbow. Time has turned aside from the smoky days of Winston Churchill.

Secretaries forced to inhale their boss's fumes would emerge enriched by lawsuits, which is no bad thing. But the cigar and all that it entails and symbolizes – conversation and camaraderie, comfort and contentment – will not go gentle into that good night.

Before I take my leave of Churchill's cigar, I thought it only fitting to perform a pilgrimage, to visit once more the back room of J.J. Fox and Robert Lewis (as it is now known), where the great leather-bound ledgers that detail Churchill's consumption in a copper-plate hand still rest, to sit on the worn and creaking leather chair constructed with brass studs, where he sat on rare visits to the store. As I eased myself down on to the chair, it was as if time had folded over and I was, however briefly, able to enjoy Churchill's company – not the domineering and sparkling conversationalist but the quiet, reflective side of this man who found solutions in billows of smoke. Yet the illusion quickly dispersed.

Framed behind glass is the box of twenty-five Romeo y Julieta cigars which were dropped in the garden of Chartwell in the summer of 1964. Today they are brown, cracked and crinkled with age, unsmokeable on grounds both of value and of taste, but still a link to the great man.

Yet it is in Chartwell that one feels closest to the spirit of Winston Churchill. The small brick studio which he helped to construct brick by brick, and where he retired to paint, is the resting place for the mahogany cabinet laden with cigars, presented by the Cuban Government. Once Churchill had emptied it of smokes he then filled it with Swiss, German and French oil paints. The ashtray he used while painting was another gift, made from the casing of a three-inch rocket shell to commemorate the millionth shell made. The rooms of the house are scattered with mementos of cigars such as the gold fish humidor with the blue and green lilies or the three boxes on a polished wooden table, one of twenty-five Epicure Grande De Luxe Romeo y Julieta, 'exclusively imported by Robert Lewis, made in Savara, Cuba' and two more boxes of Camacho Churchills which rest under lids emblazoned with the Union Jack.

Under glass, in a display of gifts, there was the cigar box with a silver relief of Rembrandt's *The Night Watch*, which was presented in 1946 in Rotterdam; the ebony cigar box with the silver lid, presented in 1954 by the Ancient and Honourable Artillery Company of Massachusetts, USA, with an engraving which reads: 'To Whom Anglo-American Friendship owes so much.'

Chartwell, like all National Trust buildings, is strictly non-smoking, so it was to the garden that I retired. There I sat on a simple wooden bench overlooking the Weald of Kent, the soft undulating countryside so beloved of its owner. On a warm September day babies were crying in plastic pushchairs; a man in white chinos and a pale blue polyester jacket was taking a photograph; in the distance a loudspeaker played a medley of 1940s show tunes. Though slight, the breeze carried an air of melancholy. The past seemed more distant than usual. Good men, like good times, are permeable and though Winston Churchill lasted so very long, still, to ash we all must turn.

After the third attempt the match flared, my cigar caught and smoke once more began to perfume the air.

NOTES ON SOURCES

Churchill's Cigar is, perhaps, one of the more obscure books on the life and times of Winston Churchill, of which there are more than a few. However, it is based on original research and although I chose not to scatter the text with many footnotes I felt it was important to detail the source of the material. I spoke, less a formal interview than a brief chat, with Mary Soames, Winston Churchill's daughter, and interviewed at greater length Winston S. Churchill, his grandson. Among his former staff I interviewed the following: Anthony Montague Browne, Patrick Kinna, Lady Williams, Elizabeth Nel and Doreen Pugh.

The Prologue was the result of a visit to 'The Big Smoke' in Las Vegas in 2004, and the figures for cigar production and supply were taken from the December 2002 issue of *Cigar Aficionado*.

Chapter 1: The Story of Robert Lewis, Cigar Merchants, is told at greater length, and with much charm, in *A Puff of Smoke* by Iain Scarlet, published by the shop to celebrate its 200th anniversary in 1987. The history of tobacco and cigar production is explored in *The Illustrated History of Cigars* by Bernard Le Roy and Maurice Szafran (Harold Starke, 1993), while for a greater understanding of the role of tobacco I would direct you to *La Diva Nicotina, The Story of How Tobacco Seduced the World* by Iain Gately (Scribner, 2002). The early life of Winston Churchill is explored in *From Winston with Love and Kisses: The Young Churchill* by Celia Sandys (Sinclair-Stevenson, 1994).

Chapter 2: Humidor & Home. The portrait of Dunhill was drawn from information taken from the Dunhill archive, while the correspondence between Winston Churchill, his secretary and the various cigar companies was drawn from the Churchill Archive at Cambridge University.

Chapter 3: Protecting the Prime Minister. The sections dealing with Doctor Roche Lynch are drawn from correspondence between the principal parties, to be found in the Churchill Archives. The actual files are under Char

2/434 and those of particular assistance run from Char 2/434/2 to Char 2/434/139. The subject was first tackled by Allan Packwood in his essay, 'Protecting the premier' in his Finest Hour 106.

Chapter 4: The Churchill Cigar. The correspondence between Senator Carter Glass and Winston Churchill can be found in the Churchill Archives in the files Char 2/419/100, while the correspondence with Samuel Kaplan is in Char 2/466/14–26, also in Char 2/494/50–75 and Char 2/532/54–75. The theft of cigars from the batch presented to Churchill is detailed in correspondence Char 2/563/106–116.

Chapter 5: His Man In Havana. The description of Churchill's visit to Cuba is drawn from the accounts in Havana newspapers such as *El Mundo* and *Diario De La Marina* from February 1946, as well as reports in *The Times* of London. This is supported by an interview with Jorge J. Fernandez, who worked at the Hotel Nacional during Churchill's visit. Antonio Giraudier wrote a vast number of letters to Winston Churchill between 1946 and Churchill's death in 1965. They are located at the Churchill Archive in the following files: Char 2/159; Char 2/218 and Char 2/524.

Chapter 6: Winston Churchill's relationship with Australia is described in much greater detail in *Man of the Century: Winston Churchill and his Legend since 1945* by John Ramsden (HarperCollins, 2002); the details of the Churchill 'Cigar' are drawn from correspondence with the local library. Further information on the reaction to Joe Orton's play *What the Butler Saw* can be found in John Lahr's fine biography, *Prick Up Your Ears* (Allen Lane, 1978). The extensive array of Churchilliana is detailed in *The Book of Churchilliana* by Douglas Hall (New Cavendish Books, 2002).

BIBLIOGRAPHY

Adamic, Louis, *Dinner at the White House* (Harper & Brothers, 1946).

Browne, Anthony Montague, *Long Sunset: Memoirs of Winston Churchill's Last Private Secretary* (Cassell Publishers, 1995).

Chase, Simon, *Cultivating a tradition of Perfection: An Enthusiast's Guide To Habanos* (Habanos).

Churchill, R.S., *Winston S. Churchill*, Vol. 1: *Youth: 1874–1900* (Heinemann, 1966).

– *Winston S. Churchill*, Vol. II: *Young Statesman, 1900–14* (Heinemann, 1967).

Gately, Iain, *La Diva Nicotina: The Story of How Tobacco Seduced The World* (Scribner, 2002).

Gilbert, Martin, *Continue to Pester, Nag and Bite: Churchill's War Leadership* (Vintage Canada, 2004).

– *In Search of Churchill* (HarperCollins, 1994).

– *Winston S. Churchill*, Vol. III: *The Challenge of War, 1914–16* (Heinemann, 1971).

– *Winston S. Churchill*, Vol. IV: *The Stricken World, 1917–22* (Heinemann, 1975).

– *Winston S. Churchill*, Vol. V: *The Prophet of Truth, 1922–39* (Heinemann, 1976).

– *Winston S. Churchill*, Vol. VI: *Their Finest Hour, 1939–41*, (Heinemann, 1983).

– *Winston S. Churchill*, Vol. VII: *The Road to Victory, 1941–45* (Heinemann, 1986).

– *Winston S. Churchill*, Vol. VIII: *Never Despair: 1945–65* (Heinemann, 1988).

Gott, Richard, *Cuba: A New History* (Yale Nota Bene, 2005).

Hall, Douglas, *The Book of Churchilliana* (New Cavendish Books, 2002).

Jenkins, Roy, *Churchill: A Biography* (Macmillan, 2001).

Infante, Guillermo Cabrera, *Holy Smoke* (Overlook Press, 1998).

Keegan, John, *Churchill* (Weidenfeld & Nicolson, 2002).

Le Roy, Bernard, & Szafran, Maurice, *The Illustrated History of Cigars* (Harold Starke, 1993).

BIBLIOGRAPHY

Manchester, William, *The Last Lion: Winston Spencer Churchill, Visions of Glory, 1874–1932* (Little, Brown, 1983).

– *The Last Lion: Winston Spencer Churchill, Alone, 1932–1940* (Little, Brown, 1988).

Meacham, Jon, *Franklin & Winston, A Portrait of a Friendship* (Granta Books, 2004)

Ramsden, John, *Man of the Century: Winston Churchill and His Legend since 1945* (HarperCollins, 2002).

Reynolds, David, *In Command of History, Churchill Fighting and Writing the Second World War* (Allen Lane, 2004).

Sandys, Celia, *From Winston with Love and Kisses: The Young Churchill* (Sinclair-Stevenson, 1994).

Thomas, Hugh, *Cuba: The Pursuit of Freedom* (Harper & Row, 1971).

Thompson, Walter, *Assignment Churchill* (Farrar, Straus and Young, 1956).

INDEX

INDEX